EIGIL KIAER

GARDEN
FLOWERS

IN COLOUR

Illustrated by
VERNER HANCKE

Translated by
H. G. WITHAM FOGG

BLANDFORD PRESS
LONDON

PREFACE

This book is chiefly designed to help those who own a garden or who are thinking of having one. But it is also written for all those who live in town houses or in flats with little or no garden, and who desire to make themselves familiar with the marvellous flowers which can be cultivated.

They will find pleasure, in the course of their walks, in being able to identify the plants that they see, and in learning from what part of the world they originated.

The choice of the plants covered in this book has been carefully worked out by the author, Runo Löwenmo, in collaboration with the garden architect, Eigil Kiaer, of Copenhagen. The text has been translated and adapted for British readers by H. G. Witham Fogg, and certain names have been modified.

It is hoped that this book will be widely read and will stimulate interest in the many beautiful flowers to be seen growing in gardens of all sizes.

1. *Achillea filipendulina*, 'Parker's variety'
2. *Achillea millefolium*, 'Cerise Queen'
3. *Adonis vernalis*
4. *Aconitum napellus*, 'Spark's variety'
5. *Ajuga repens*

6

6

7

8

9

6. *Ageratum houstonianum*
7. *Alyssum maritimum*, 'Violet Queen'
8. *Alyssum saxatile*, 'Gold Dust'
9. *Alisma*, water plantain

10. *Althaea,* (Hollyhock) rosea
11. *Althaea,* (Hollyhock) Chater's double rose
12. *Anchusa italica,* 'Dropmore'
13. *Anchusa myosotidiflora*

8

14. *Anemone blanda*
15. *Anemone* de Caen
16. *Anemone japonica*, 'Queen Charlotte'
17. *Anemone japonica*, 'September Charm'
18. *Anthemis tinctoria*, 'Kelwayi'

19. *Antirrhinum majus*, 'Golden Dawn' – 20. *Antirrhinum majus*, 'Royal Cerise' – 21. *Antirrhinum majus*, 'Purple Eclipse' – 22. *Antirrhinum majus*, 'Welcome' – 23. *Antirrhinum majus*, 'Golden Queen' – 24. *Antirrhinum majus*, 'Defiance'

25. *Aquilegia coerulea* hybrids
26. *Aquilegia coerulea*, 'Helenae'
27. *Aquilegia coerulea*, 'Crimson Star'
28. *Aquilegia skinneri* (Mexican Columbine)

29. *Arabis caucasica* – 30. *Arabis caucasica*, double – 31. *Arabis caucasica, rosea* – 32. *Armeria maritima splendens* – 33. *Arum italicum* – 34. *Artemisia lactiflora* – 35. *Aruncus sylvester*

36. *Aster amellus*, 'October Dawn'
37. *Aster amellus*, 'Sonia'
38. *Aster sedifolius acris nanus*
39. *Aster amellus*, 'Wonder of Stafa'
40. *Aster amellus*, 'Goblin'

41. *Aster ericoides*
42. *Aster Novi - belgii,* 'Royal Blue'
43. *Aster alpinus superbus*
44. *Aster Novi - belgii,* 'Beechwood Challenger'
45. *Aster hybridus,* 'Pink Lady'

14

46

47

48

49

50

51

46. *Astilbe arendsii hybrida*, – 47. *Astilbe*, 'Fanal' – 48. *Astilbe*, 'Ceres' – 49. *Astilbe*, 'Purple Glory' – 50. *Astilbe*, 'Queen of Laughter' – 51. *Astrantia major*

52. *Aubrieta deltoides* – 53. *Aubrieta*, 'Crimson King' –
54. *Aubrieta*, 'Dr. Mules' – 55. *Aubrieta*, 'Purple Robe' –
56. *Aubrieta*, 'King Waldemar' – 57. *Aubrieta*, lavender
hybrid

58. *Begonia semperflorens*, 'Red Pearl'
59. *Begonia semperflorens*, 'Prima-Donna'
60. *Begonia semperflorens*, 'Tausendschon'
61. *Begonia semperflorens*, 'Carpet of Snow'

62. *Begonia multiflora*, 'Flamboyant'
63. *Begonia multiflora*, 'Frau Helen Harms'
64. *Begonia*, giant flowered tuberous
65. *Begonia*, 'Madame Oscar Lamarck'

66. *Bellis perennis*, 'Easter Daisy'
67. *Bellis perennis*, double flowered
68. *Bergenia cordifolia* purpurea
69. *Briza maxima*, ornamental grass
70. *Butomus umbellatus*

71. *Calceolaria integrifolia*
72. *Calceolaria polyrrhiza*
73. *Calendula officinalis*, 'Balls Orange'
74. *Calendula officinalis*, 'Balls Gold'

75. *Callistephus chinensis*, 'China' Aster
76. *Callistephus chinensis*, 'Marguerite' Aster
77. *Callistephus chinensis*, 'Ostrich Plume' Aster
78. *Callistephus chinensis*, 'Lilliput' Aster

79. *Calla palustris*
80. *Calla palustris,* double
81. *Caltha palustris,* single, 'Marsh Marigold'

82. *Canna indica,* Indian hybrids
83. *Canna indica,* Shot or speckled canna
84. *Canna indica, hybrida,* pale pink Indian hybrid

85. *Campanula carpatica* – 86. *Campanula glomerata dahurica* –
87. *Campanula media* – 88. *Campanula persicifolia* –
89. *Campanula portenschlagiana* – 90. *Campanula pusilla*

24

93

91   92

94

91. *Centaurea cyanus,* blue cornflower
92. *Centaurea Montana,* rose
93. *Centaurea Montana,* blue, rose centre
94. *Centranthus ruber, var. Coccineus*

95. *Cerastrum biebersteinii*
96. *Cheiranthus cheiri*, Wallflower
97. *Cheiranthus allionii*
98. *Chiastophyllum oppositifolium*

99.   *Chrysanthemum indicum*, 'Gold Dust'
100. *Chrysanthemum indicum*, 'Anastasia'
101. *Chrysanthemum Korean hybrid*, 'Apollo'
102. *Chrysanthemum Korean hybrid*, 'Hebe'

103. *Chrysanthemum indicum,* 'Gobelin'
104. *Chrysanthemum indicum,* 'September Gold'
105. *Chrysanthemum indicum,* 'Phoenix'
106. *Chrysanthemum indicum,* 'Madame Marie Masse'

28

107. *Chrysanthemum Coccineum, (Pyrethrum)* 'Eileen May Robinson'
108. *Chrysanthemum Coccineum, (Pyrethrum)* 'James Kelway'
109. *Chrysanthemum Maximum,* 'Universal'
110. *Chrysanthemum Coccineum, (Pyrethrum)* 'Queen Mary'

111. *Chrysanthemum segetum,* 'Eldorado'
112. *Chrysanthemum carinatum, tricolor*
113. *Chrysanthemum frutescens*
114. *Chrysanthemum coronarium*

115. *Clarkia elegans*, double mixed
116. *Cimicifuga dahurica*, 'Silver Spike'
117. *Cimicifuga racemosa*

118. *Cobaea scandens*
119. *Colchicum autumnale*
120. *Convallaria majalis*, 'Lily of the Valley'

121. *Coreopsis tinctoria,*
122. *Coreopsis verticillata grandiflora*
123. *Cosmos bipinnatus*
124. *Corydalis lutea*

125. *Crocus aureus*
126. *Crocus speciosus*
127. *Crocus vernus*
128. *Cyclamen neapolitanum*
129. *Cypripedium calceolus*

130. *Dahlia*, 'Italia'
131. *Dahlia*, single mixed
132. *Dahlia*, 'Oslo'

133. *Dahlia*, 'Helly Boudewyn'
134. *Dahlia*, 'Thor'
135. *Dahlia*, 'General Carl Moltke'
136. *Dahlia*, 'Golden Leader'
137. *Dahlia*, 'Riante'

138. *Dahlia*, 'Bacchus'
139. *Dahlia*, 'Gerrie Hoek'
140. *Dahlia*, 'Arc de Triomphe'
141. *Dahlia*, 'Troef'

142. *Dahlia*, 'Ballego's Glory'
143. *Dahlia*, 'Vermilion Brilliant'
144. *Dahlia*, 'Andries Pink'
145. *Dahlia*, 'Ahoy'
146. *Dahlia*, 'Therose'

147. *Dahlia*, 'Duindigt'
148. *Dahlia*, 'Brandaris'
149. *Dahlia*, 'Yellow Special'
150. *Dahlia*, 'Good Morning'

151. *Dahlia*, 'Fine Aniversary'
152. *Dahlia*, 'Silvoretta'.
153. *Dahlia*, 'Pin Up'
154. *Dahlia* ,'White Superior'

155. *Dahlia*, 'Bronze Elsie Crellin'
156. *Dahlia*, 'Elsie Crellin'
157. *Dahlia*, 'Baby Rose'
158. *Dahlia*, 'Freda'
159. *Dahlia*, 'Goldelse'

160. *Dahlia*, 'A propos' – 161. *Dahlia*, 'Heloise' –
162. *Dahlia*, 'Nerissa' – 163. *Dahlia*, 'Kochelse' –
164. *Dahlia*, 'Pinnochio' – 165. *Dahlia*, 'Zonnegoud'
166. *Dahlia*, 'Sonya'

167. *Dahlia*, 'Symphonia'
168. *Dahlia*, 'Snow Princess'
169. *Dahlia*, 'Light of the Moon'
170. *Dahlia*, 'Colorit'
171. *Dahlia*, 'La Cierva'

172. *Delphinium,* 'Constance'
173. *Delphinium,* 'Lamartine'
174. *Delphinium,* 'Mrs Thomson'

175
176
178
177

175. *Delphinium*, Pacific Giant Strain
176. *Delphinium ruysii*, 'Pink Sensation'
177. *Delphinium nudicaule*
178. *Delphinium*, 'Persimmon'

179. *Dianthus barbatus*
180. *Dianthus caryophyllus*, carnation
181. *Dianthus plumarius*, 'Duchess of Fife'
182. *Dianthus caryophyllus*, 'Countess Knuth'
183. *Dianthus plumarius*, 'Diamant'

184. *Dicentra spectabilis*
185. *Dimorphotheca aurantiaca*
186. *Digitalis purpurea*

187. *Dodecatheon meadia*
188. *Doronicum,* 'Mrs Mason'
189. *Dryas octopetala*
190. *Echinops ritro*

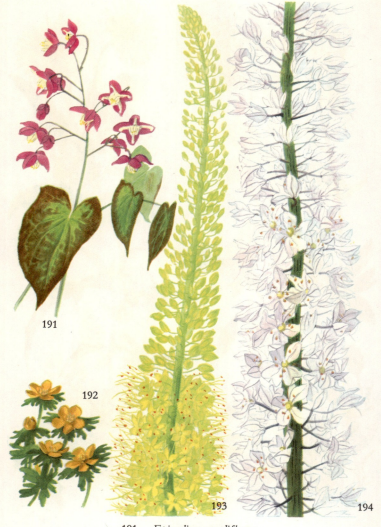

191. *Epimedium grandiflorum*
192. *Eranthis hiemalis*
193. *Eremurus bungei*
194. *Eremurus robustus*

195. *Erigeron speciosum*, 'Wupperthal'
196. *Erigeron hybridum*, 'Quakeress'
197. *Erigeron hybridum*, 'Summer Snow'
198. *Erigeron speciosum, mesa-grande*

199. *Eryngium hybridum*
200. *Erythronium dens-canis*
201. *Eschscholtzia californica*

202. *Euphorbia*, yellow spurge
203. *Filipendulina (spiraea) venusta*
204. *Filipendulina (spiraea) hexapetala*

205. *Fritillaria imperialis*
206. *Galanthus nivalis*
207. *Fritillaria meleagris*

208
209
210
211

208. *Gaillardia grandiflora*
209. *Galega officinalis*
210. *Gentiana acaulis*
211. *Geranium endressii*

212. *Geum heldreichii*
213. *Geum*, 'Mrs. Bradshaw'
214. *Geum*, 'Lady Stratheden'
215. *Gladiolus*, large flowered hybrids

216. *Godetia*, 'Sybil Sherwood'
217. *Gypsophila elegans*
218. *Gypsophila paniculata*

56

219. *Helenium,* 'Crimson Beauty'
220. *Helenium pumilum magnificum*
221. *Helenium,* 'Chipperfield Orange'
222. *Helenium,* 'Moerheim Beauty'

223. *Helianthus bismarckianus*
224. *Helianthus annuus*
225. *Helianthus rigidis*

226. *Helichrysum bracteatum*
227. *Heliopsis, scabra patula*
228. *Heliotropium peruvianum*

229. *Helleborus abchasicus*
230. *Helleborus niger*, 'Christmas Rose'
231. *Hemerocallis hybridus*

232. *Hesperis matronalis*
233. *Hepatica*, 'Hungarian anemone'
234. *Hepatica triloba*, double rose
235. *Heuchera brizoides*

236. *Hosta ventricosa*
237. *Hosta lancifolia*

238.   *Hyacinth,* 'Lady Derby'
239.   *Hyacinth,* 'La Victoire'
240.   *Hyacinth,* 'Queen of the Pinks'

241   242   243

241.   *Hyacinth*, 'City of Haarlem'
242.   *Hyacinth*, 'Grand Maitre'
243.   *Hyacinth*, 'L'Innocence'

244. *Iberis*, 'Snowflake'
245. *Iberis, umbellata purpurea*
246. *Impatiens balsamina*
247. *Incarvillea delavayi*
248. *Ipomaea purpurea*

249. *Iris pumila*
250. *Iris pseudacorus*
251. *Iris reticulata*
252. *Iris siberica*

253. *Iris germanica*, 'Madame Chereau'
254. *Iris germanica*, 'Madame Gaudichau'
255. *Iris germanica*, 'Clematis'
256. *Iris germanica*, 'Flamboyant'
257. *Iris germanica, odoratissima*

258. *Iris germanica*, 'La Beaute'
259. *Iris germanica*, 'Mrs Neubrunner'
260. *Iris germanica*, 'Rota'
261. *Iris germanica*, 'Rheine Traube'

262. *Kniphofia*, 'The Rocket'
263. *Kniphofia*, 'Royal Standard'
264. *Kochia trichophylla*

265. *Lathyrus odoratus,* 'Sweet Pea'
266. *Lathyrus latifolius*
267. *Lathyrus vernus*

268. *Lavatera trimestris*
269. *Leontopodium alpinum*, Edelweiss
270. *Leucojum vernum*
271. *Liatris spicata*

272. *Lilium candidum*
273. *Lilium martagon*
274. *Lilium regale*

275. *Lilium tigrinum*
276. *Lilium umbellatum*, 'Darkest of all'
277. *Lilium umbellatum*, 'Golden Fleece'

278. *Linaria pallida*
279. *Linum perenne*
280. *Linum grandiflorum*
281. *Lobelia erinus*
282. *Lobelia hybrida pendula* (trailing)

283

283. *Lupinus polyphyllus,* mixed

284. *Lychnis chalcedonica* (Jerusalem Cross)
285. *Lychnis coronaria*
286. *Lysimachia nummularia*
287. *Lysimachia punctata*

288. *Lythrum salicaria*, 'Rose Queen'
289. *Macleaya (Bocconia) cordata*
290. *Malope trifida*
291. *Matricaria eximia*

292. *Matthiola incana annua*, 'Ten Week Stock'
293. *Mimulus cupreus*
294. *Mimulus tigrinus hybridus*

295
296
297

295. *Meconopsis betonicifolia*
296. *Menyanthes trifoliata*
297. *Montbretia crocosmiiflora*

298. *Monarda didyma*, 'Cambridge Scarlet'
299. *Myosotis sylvatica*
300. *Myosotis palustris*
301. *Muscari botryoides*

302. *Narcissus tazzetta*
303. *Narcissus poetaz*, 'Scarlet Gem'
304. *Narcissus poetaz*, 'Laurens Koster'
305. *Narcissus poeticus*, 'Actaea'
306. *Narcissus*, 'Scarlet Elegance'

307. *Narcissus*, 'Golden Harvest'
308. *Narcissus*, 'Spring Glory'
309. *Narcissus*, 'Van Sion'

310. *Nemesia Strumosa*, mixed
311. *Nemesia insignis*
312. *Nepeta Mussini*
313. *Nicotiana Sanderae*
314. *Nigella damascena*

315. *Nymphaea,* 'James Brydon'
316. *Nymphaea alba*
317. *Nymphaea marliacea,* 'Chromatella'
318. *Nymphaea,* 'Escarboucle'

319. *Oenothera glauca*, 'Fraseri'
320. *Oenothera missouriensis*
321. *Omphalodes verna*
322. *Ornithogalum nutans*

323. *Paeonia albiflora*, 'MacMahon'
324. *Paeonia*, 'Queen Wilhelmina'
325. *Paeonia*, 'Couronne d'Or'
326. *Paeonia officinalis*, double rose
327. *Paeonia officinalis*, double red

328. *Paeonia albiflora*, 'Kashna-no-Mai'
329. *Paeonia albiflora*, 'Kasugano'
330. *Paeonia albiflora*, 'Whitleyi Major'
331. *Paeonia albiflora*, 'Avalanche'

332. *Papaver nudicaule,* Iceland Poppy
333. *Papaver orientale,* Oriental Poppy
334. *Papaver somniferum,* (Opium Poppy)
335. *Papaver somniferum,* 'Dannebrog'

336. *Pelargonium peltatum*, 'Cattleya'
337. *Pelargonium peltatum*, 'Madame Crousse'
338. *Pelargonium peltatum*, 'Balkan King'
339. *Pelargonium peltatum*, *rubra robusta*

340. *Pelargonium zonale,* 'Meteor'
341. *Pelargonium zonale,* 'West Brighton Gem'
342. *Pelargonium zonale,* 'Purple King'

343. *Pelargonium zonale*, 'Leif'
344. *Pelargonium zonale*, 'Poitevine Beauty'
345. *Pelargonium zonale*, 'Madame Salleron'

346. *Penstemon gentianoides hybrida*
347. *Petunia,* 'Rose of Heaven'
348. *Petunia,* 'Lavender Blue'
349. *Petunia violacea*
350. *Petunia,* 'Canadian Wonder'

351. *Phlox drummondii* mixed
352. *Phlox paniculata*, 'Frau Alfred von Mauthner'
353. *Phlox paniculata*, 'Amethyst'
354. *Phlox paniculata*, 'Jules Sandeau'

355. *Phlox paniculata*, 'Riverton Jewel'
356. *Phlox paniculata*, 'Evelyn'
357. *Phlox paniculata*, 'Hindenburg'
358. *Phlox paniculata*, 'Fritiof'

359. *Phlox paniculata*, 'Mia Ruys'
360. *Phlox paniculata*, 'Wilhelm Kesselring'
361. *Phlox paniculata*, 'Queen's Cluster'

362. *Phlox subulata nivalis*
363. *Phlox subulata atropurpurea*
364. *Phlox subulata,* 'G. F. Wilson'
365. *Phlox subulata,* 'Lilacina'

366. *Physostegia virginiana*
367. *Phytolacca americana*
368. *Polemonium coeruleum*
369. *Polemonium reptans*

370. *Polygonatum multiflorum*
371. *Polygonum bistorta*
372. *Potentilla*, 'Gibson's Scarlet'
373. *Potentilla aurea*
374. *Potentilla*, 'Miss Willmott'

375. *Primula beesiana*
376. *Primula denticulata*
377. *Primula florindae*
378. *Primula hortensis*

379. *Primula japonica*
380. *Primula Sieboldii*
381. *Primula pulverulenta*, 'Helenae'
382. *Primula*, 'Wanda'
383. *Primula variabilis*

384. *Pulmonaria angustifolia*, 'Mrs Moon'
385. *Pulsatilla vulgaris*
386. *Reseda odorata*, Mignonette
387. *Ranunculus asiaticus*

388. *Ricinus communis*
389. *Rodgersià aesculifolia*
390. *Rodgersia tabularis*

391. *Rudbeckia,* 'Herbstsonne'
392. *Rudbeckia speciosa*
393. *Rudbeckia purpurea,* 'The King'

103

394. *Sagittaria sagittifolia*
395. *Salpiglossis sinuata*
396. *Salvia nemorosa*

397. *Salvia patens*
398. *Salvia splendens*
399. *Sanvitalia procumbens*
400. *Saponaria ocymoides*

401. *Saxifraga lingulata superba*
402. *Saxifraga apiculata*
403. *Saxifraga*, 'Beauty of Ronsdorf'
404. *Saxifraga cotyledon purpurata*
405. *Saxifraga umbrosa*, London Pride

406. *Scabiosa caucasica*
407. *Scabiosa atropurpurea hybrida*

408. *Schizanthus wisetonensis*
409. *Scilla campanulata*
410. *Scilla siberica*

411. *Sedum acre*, Stone-crop
412. *Sedum ewersii*
413. *Sedum spectabile*, 'Brilliant'
414. *Sedum spathulifolium*

415. *Sedum spurium*
416. *Sedum*, 'Munstead Dark Red'. Large flowered Stone-
crop

417. *Sempervivum arachnoideum*
418. *Sempervivum heuffelii*
419. *Sempervivum funckii*
420. *Sempervivum tectorum alpinum*

421. *Senecio przewalskii*
422. *Sidalcea*, 'Elsie Hugh'

423   424

425

423.   *Solidago*, 'Golden Veil' (Golden Rod)
424.   *Solidago*, 'Golden Wings'
425.   *Solidago*, 'Perkeo'

426. *Stachys macrantha*
427. *Stachys lanata*
428. *Stachys sinuata*
429. *Statice latifolia* (Limonium)

430. *Tagetes patula nana*, 'Robert Beist'
431. *Tagetes patula nana*, lemon-yellow
432. *Tagetes erecta*, 'Yellow Supreme'
433. *Tagetes erecta*, 'Guinea Gold'

434. *Tagetes patula*, 'Naughty Marietta'
435. *Tagetes patula*, 'Harmony' (French Marigold)
436. *Tagetes*, 'Flash'
437. *Tagetes signata pumila*

438. *Thalictrum aquilegifolium*
439. *Thalictrum dipterocarpum*
440. *Thymus serphyllum splendens*
441. *Thymus lanuginosus*

442. *Tradescantia virginiana*
443. *Trollius europaeus superbus*
444. *Trollius*, 'Orange Globe'
445. *Trollius*, 'Prichards Giant'

446. *Tropaeolum majus* (Nasturtium)
447. *Tropaeolum,* double
448. *Tropaeolum,* 'King of Tom Thumb'
449. *Tropaeolum peregrinum*

450. *Tulipa fosteriana,* 'Red Emperor'
451. *Tulipa Kaufmanniana*
452. *Tulipa praestans,* 'Fusilier'

453. *Tulip* single, 'Ibis'
454. *Tulip* single, 'Keizerskroon'
455. *Tulip* single, 'Couleur Cardinal'
456. *Tulip* single, 'Yellow Prince'
457. *Tulip* single, 'Brilliant Star'

458. *Tulip* double, 'Peach Blossom'
459. *Tulip* double, 'Therose'
460. *Tulip* double, 'Orange Nassau'

461. *Tulip* Darwin, 'Clara Butt'
462. *Tulip* Darwin, 'Demeter'
463. *Tulip* Darwin, 'Golden Age'
464. *Tulip* Cottage, 'Aristocrat'
465. *Tulip* Darwin, 'William Pitt'
466. *Tulip* Darwin, 'City of Haarlem'

467. *Tulip* Darwin, 'Scarlet Leader'
468. *Tulip* Darwin, 'The Bishop'
469. *Tulip* Darwin, 'Pride of Zwanenburg'
470. *Tulip* Darwin, 'Zwanenburg'
471. *Tulip* Darwin, 'Afterglow'
472. *Tulip* Darwin, 'La Tulipe Noire'

473. *Tulip* Cottage, 'Golden Harvest' – 474. *Tulip* Cottage, 'Louis XIV' – 475. *Tulip* Cottage, 'Princess Margaret Rose' – 476. *Tulip* Cottage, 'Telescopium' – 477. *Tulip* Cottage, 'Orange Wonder' – 478. *Tulip* Cottage, 'Dillenburg' – 479. *Tulip* Cottage, 'Mona Lucia'

480. *Tulip* Lily flowered, 'Captain Fryatt'
481. *Tulip* Lily flowered, 'Mrs Moon'
482. *Tulip* Parrot, 'Violet Queen'
483. *Tulip* Parrot, 'Sunshine'
484. *Tulip* Parrot, 'Red Champion'

485. *Verbascum phoeniceum*, 'Pink Domino'
486. *Verbascum olympicum*

487. *Verbena*, 'Defiance'
488. *Verbena*, 'Royal Blue'
489. *Verbena candidissima*
490. *Verbena venosa*, hybrids.
491. *Verbena*, 'Dannebrog'

492. *Veronica incana*
493. *Veronica spicata*, 'Erika'
494. *Veronica longifolia*
495. *Veronica teucrium*, 'Royal Blue'

496. *Viola cornuta*, 'Hansa'
497. *Viola gracilis*, 'Lord Nelson'
498. *Viola hybrida*, 'Aurora'
499. *Viola hybrida*, 'Jackanapes'
500. *Viola odorata*, (Violet)

501. *Viola tricolor,* 'Jupiter' Large flowered Pansy – 502. *Viola tricolor,* 'Iskunger' Large flowered Pansy – 503 *Viola tricolor,* Large flowered Pansy – 504. *Viola tricolor,* 'Mars' Large flowered Pansy – 505. *Viola tricolor,* Large flowered Pansy – 506. *Viola tricolor,* Large flowered Pansy – 507. *Viola tricolor,* 'Roggli' Large flowered Pansy

508.   *Viscaria splendens, flore pleno*
509.   *Yucca filamentosa*

510. *Zinnia elegans* mixed
511. *Zinnia*, 'Lilliput' mixed

NOMENCLATURE, BIOLOGY
AND CULTIVATION

THE notes which follow are numbered to correspond with the flowers illustrated in the first part of the book. A few varieties which are not illustrated, but which are remarkable for various reasons, have also been mentioned in the text.

Each species, variety or plant hybrid is given its horticultural designation, by which it is internationally known. The names of the genus and species are in Latin; the names of the varieties are either in Latin or in the native language of the creator of the variety. One finds, for example, *Iberis umbellata purpurea* and *Iris germanica*, 'La Beaute'. The name of the plant is usually accompanied by one or two of its most commonly used names.

Among the plants are those descending directly from the natural species, but which have been modified to some degree by culture and selection, and others resulting from the crossing between two species or even from the crossing of a fertile hybrid with another species.

The ecological requirements of the plants in cultivation as regards climate, soil etc. approximate to those of the natural parent species. It has therefore seemed helpful to indicate the country of origin. The information concerning the habit, height of the plant, diameter of the flowers and date of flowering etc. are given as an average. These details can differ considerably according to the locality (geographical situation, altitude, aspect and exposure), and to the conditions of soil, humidity and light.

From these notes can be determined the conditions which are the most favourable for cultivation, propagation, transplanting and positioning. Although brief, they contain information about the various species which, it is felt, will be of interest to amateur growers.

DESCRIPTIVE AND CULTURAL NOTES

1-2 Achillea *(Yarrow)*

The name of this genus recalls the Greek warrior, Achilles, who, according to mythology, was accustomed to use decorations of this plant in order to be in form for his warlike feats. The genus, *Achillea*, comprises in the temperate regions about 80 perfumed species among which are a few alpine plants. *A. millefolium*, well-known medicinal plant, and *A. ptarmica* are very frequently met with. Achilleas endure drought very well and can be cultivated in a variety of soils. They do well in a good position and prefer the full sun.

1 Achillea filipendulina
'*Parker's variety*'

Plant for border display and for flowers to cut; attains 5 ft in height; flowers from June to October, making really bushy plants. Colour: bright yellow which is retained in drying. Native of Caucasus.

2 Achillea millefolium *(Milfoil)*
'*Cerise Queen*'

Milfoil is frequently found in this country. The variety with rose-coloured flowers, 'Cerise Queen', is cultivated and there are varieties having flowers which are nearly red, such as 'Kelwayi' and 'Crimson Beauty'. Favourable effects are obtained by placing them in a border or a rock garden. In good soil, the plants attain a height of 20 ins. Diameter of the flowers 2-4 ins. Length of flowering, mid-June to September. The richness in bitter substances of milfoil makes it a rare medicinal plant.

3 Adonis vernalis *(Pheasant's Eye)*

This perennial plant, which flowers in April-May, is most ornamental for gardens and rockeries; its fragile attractive foliage harmonises well with its lemon-yellow flowers. It attains a height of from 8-10 ins. and its flowers have a diameter of from 1½-2½ ins. Cultivate it in a sunny position, keeping the roots moist during flowering. It prefers a soil rich in lime. Do not transplant it too early. The leaves fade in August. Propagate by division in the autumn. Grows abundantly in the Pyrenees and in many other parts of Europe.

4 Aconitum napellus *(Monk's Hood,* '*Spark's variety*'

A native species in Europe and in Asia. It is one of our oldest garden plants. A plant resulting from the crossing of *Aconitum napellus* with *A. stoerekianum* is generally cultivated. Every part of the plant contains a strong poison, aconitine, which however will not be harmful if the plants are handled in the ordinary way.

'Spark's variety' attains a height of about 5 ft; it is considered one of the most valuable hybrids by reason of its late flowering. Mention must be made of other varieties of horticultural value including *A. n. album*; *A. n. albo-roseum* (white and rose); *A. n. bicolor* (white and blue lilac); *A. n. carneum* (bright red). A well-manured soil and partial shade will produce magnificent specimens.

5 Ajuga repens *(Bugle)*

Thirty species of *Ajuga* exist, inhabiting the Ancient World and Australia. *A. reptans* reproduces itself by the creeping shoots put out by its stem. It is as happy in the sun as in the shade.

provided the moisture is sufficient. However, certain varieties with coloured leaves should be cultivated in the sun including *A. r. fol. var.* (leaves speckled with white); *A. r. purpureus* (red leaves) and *A. r. multicolor* (multicoloured). Excellent for the rockery and as a ground cover for small bushes and roses. Flowers from April-May until August. Height of the plant 4-6 ins.

6 Ageratum houstonianum
(Floss Flower)

Plant of Mexican origin; perennial, but treated as an annual in the garden. Do not transplant until the end of the frosts. The plant is often in flower at the time of transplanting and its flowering continues until the autumn frosts, provided the faded flowers are removed. The plant is usually reproduced by seeds, but to preserve certain characteristics from one year to another it is necessary to propagate by cuttings. Few plants in our country flower as well or are better suited for borders and low baskets. Height 6-12 ins. Space 8 ins. apart. Sunny aspect. Rich and light soil.

7 Alyssum maritimum '*Violet Queen*'
(Madwort or Sweet Alyssum)

A maritime cruciferous plant from the South of Europe on the coasts of the Mediterranean and the Atlantic. A perennial, but usually cultivated like an annual in the garden. Sows itself freely. Space at intervals of 4 ins. Flowers from July until the end of October. Height 4-8 ins. Suitable for borders.

8 Alyssum saxatile '*Gold Dust*'

Plant growing commonly from Germany to Asia Minor, sometimes naturalised on old walls; one of the most ornamental species of our flower gardens and rockeries. Must be renewed every 2 or 3 years, which is very easy, since the plant resows itself freely. A single plant of 3 years' growth will often be as much as 16 ins. in diameter if it finds a suitable position. 'Gold Dust' grows well in dry and poor soils and easily pushes between stones and over walls. It flowers during April and May.

9 Alisma *(Water Plantain)*

As its name indicates, this is a water plant. It prefers shallow water, but prospers also in boggy soil. Once established it gives an extraordinary impression of exuberance. Especially suitable around the edges of lakes, rivers, and streams. It blooms from June to September; the flower stems attain 32 ins. in height. It is to be found in many districts.

10 Althaea *rosea*
(Hollyhock)

Common in Asia Minor and having a wide area of distribution in Europe, hollyhocks easily become naturalised. Though a perennial, the hollyhock is frequently cultivated as a biennial. Some plants produce single flowers, others double. There are strains and varieties with petals that are flat, wavy, ruffled or fringed, etc. Colours are very varied: plain white, yellow, red, rose, violet, purple, dark brown. Blue flowers, however, are not known. Hollyhocks are obtained from seeds, by splitting roots, or by taking cuttings. The practice of grafting is rarely carried out. This subject grows well in a good depth of soil and often in poor ground, and thrives in seaside places.

11 Althaea: *Chater's double rose*
(Hollyhock)

Of Scottish origin, and considered the most beautiful of hollyhocks, this variety which is relatively low in height (about 5 ft), is very often used in borders of perennial plants. The flowers are of a great variety of colours, and generally bloom the second year after sowing. A useful flower for cutting from the end of June.

12 Anchusa italica *(Alkanet)*
'*Dropmore*'

Grows in almost the whole of Britain in the fields, and on the lime hills. The flowers are generally of a very beautiful blue. It owes its common name of 'Ox-tongue' to its leaves which are covered with stiff bristles. In good soil, well drained, a single plant easily attains a diameter of 5 ft and a height of 50 ins. It loves the sun, and resists drought well. Flowers from May until August. To avoid rotting at the neck, cut back the plant to ground level after flowering. Adventitious eyes develop, which will enter into vegetation the following spring.

13 Anchusa myosotidiflora

Small bugloss, rarely exceeding 16 ins. in height, producing azure-blue flowers in abundance bringing to mind those of myosotis. A perennial, it will grow in all types of soil but prefers half-shaded positions. Flowers from March to May. A short time after the flowers have died, the foliage fades away and must be cut off. A good flower for the garden, but not suitable for cutting.

14-17 Anemone *(Windflower)*

A genus comprising about 150 species dispersed in the two hemispheres, from the plains to the mountains in temperate regions. Certain of these species have been introduced into our gardens, for example, *Anemone nemorosa,* whose hybrids with the other species produce flowers shaded with blue and rose.

14 Anemone blanda

Height 6-8 ins. Flowers from April to May. It will grow in sunshine or half-shade. Has been used for the production of hybrids with white, blue or red flowers. It prefers light soils, rich in humus, and is particularly suitable for growing on grassy slopes, rockeries and under the shade of trees.

15 Anemone
de Caen

In cultivation for a very long time, this anemone is unquestionably one of our most beautiful of ornamental plants. Its corms can be preserved dry for two years. It resists the cold quite well, but if it is planted in autumn it benefits from a covering of decayed leaves. It dislikes too much moisture in winter. As a precaution against possible loss, it is advisable to plant a few new corms each year. The flower will reach 12 or more inches above the soil. When cut, it lasts a very long time. Flowering from the beginning of spring, it will often go on blooming until autumn. Colours very varied and intense.

16 Anemone japonica
'*Queen Charlotte*'

These autumn anemones, or anemones from Japan, add an oriental flavour to the garden. They are very beautiful plants, forming clumps with flowering stems which attain a height of 2 ft. To obtain a still more decorative effect, they can be planted near shorter plants. They flower from the beginning of July until the frosty season, and should be planted in sunny or in half shady positions. These anemones are sometimes sensitive to frosts, so it seems advisable to cover them with branches or dead leaves in winter.

17 Anemone japonica
'*September Charm*'

A very beautiful hybrid. Height 30 ins

18 Anthemis tinctoria 'Kelwayi'
(Ox-eye Chamomile)

Also named *Cota tinctoria* or Bull's Eye, this subject is native of Europe. The variety 'Kelwayi', with most intense colour, is cultivated in gardens and its flowers attain 2½ ins. in diameter. It is often used in borders with good exposure, where the soil is too dry for other perennial plants. Height 27 ins. Flowering June-August. A second crop of blooms can be obtained by cutting the first flowers once they begin to fade.

19-24 Antirrhinum majus
(Snapdragon)

Perennial plant growing on arid hills and rocks and which often makes its home on old walls. Cultivated as an annual, biennial or perennial. Numerous varieties are known in a very wide range of colours; flowers are often striped. The tall varieties, (24-40 ins.) are most useful for borders; the semi-dwarf ones measure from 10-16 ins.; the dwarfs from 6-10 ins. form edges for beds and borders.

They like well exposed and well-manured soils. Some watering is often necessary during dry summers. They can stand up to frost at nights without any harm. By sowing very early and transplanting in a greenhouse or under a frame, more abundant flowering and better developed plants can be obtained. Sow in an open space, or preferably in a nursery bed.

Seed firms often include many of their own special varieties in their collections The choice of this or that variety is of less importance than being able to suit height and colour to the use for which the plants are required.

25-28 Aquilegia (Columbine)

Perennial plants, the Columbines cross each other so easily that there now exists an incalculable number of hybrids. All soils suit them, but they prefer rich land and get on best in partial shade.

25 Aquilegia coerulea
hybrids

Large wide open flowers in pastel shades with or without spurs. Flowering in June. Height 28 ins. The effect will be more successful if planted in groups.

26 Aquilegia coerulea
'Helenae'

A result of crossing between *A. coerulea* and *A. flabellata nana*. Flowers about 15 days earlier than *A. coerulea*. Height 16 ins. Hardy.

27 Aquilegia coerulea
'Crimson Star'

Flowers with predominant, long red spurs. Height 28 ins. Flowering June.

28 Aquilegia skinneri
Mexican Columbine

A little more sensitive than the other varieties and so should be protected during winter. Flowers, July-August, with neatly designed spurs. Height 24 ins.

29 Arabis caucasica (Rock Cress)

Of Caucasian origin. A perennial which forms a carpet as it grows and is suitable for rockeries. Flowering April-May. Height 6 ins.

30 Arabis caucasica
double

Grows rapidly, needs space and is equally suited to all soils. Grows well in sunny rockeries. Height of the foliage 6 ins.; of the flowering plant 10 ins. Perennial. The flowers, when cut, keep well in a vase and make one think of little gilliflowers (stocks). Do not reproduce from seed if it is desired to preserve the characteristics of the variety.

31 Arabis caucasica *rosea*

Shorter than the previous variety. This resows itself. It is best to eliminate the strains originating from the seeds which do not reproduce themselves true to type.

32 Armeria maritima splendens (*Thrift*)

This plant from the grassy slopes and cliffs of the ocean and channel coasts can be cultivated easily in poor soil and in the full sun. It is, on this account, very valuable in establishing dwarf perennial edgings. The tufts reach a height of 2 ins. and remain green even during winter. It flowers from May until July. The stems of the flowers grow to a height of 6 ins. To preserve the tufts in a good state, transplant them every 3 or 4 years.

33 Arum italicum (*Italian Arum*)

Grows naturally in several European countries. Leaves are produced before winter, in a spearhead veined in white. From the first day of spring, a large whitish spathe surrounds the flowers and fleshy axis, formed from various rings of flowers and ending with a butter-yellow club. The red berries ripen in July. It can serve to decorate the undergrowth in shrubberies, but is also tolerant of full light.

34 Artimesia lactiflora

Native of the East of Tibet and of the West of China. Perennial. Hardy. Grows easily, no matter what sort of soil so long as it is well drained. Useful in borders or on its own. Height about 5 ft. Flowering September-October. The flowers, when cut, keep well.

35 Aruncus sylvester (*Goat's Beard*)

Grows wild in the humid woods of hilly places. Perennial. Small white flowers in large, elegant panicles. The male forms are the most sought after, as they are more decorative. Height 60-80 ins. Does not need a support. Flowers in June-July. After flowering, cut the dead flowers; the foliage will remain fresh all the summer. It will grow well anywhere, but prefers moist soils.

36-45 Aster (*Michaelmas Daisy*)

All the asters listed are perennial. They like the sun and prefer rich soils. Certain species tend to make a lot of growth and it is necessary to divide them fairly often. Species, varieties and hybrids are very numerous.

36 Aster amellus
'*October Dawn*'

The word *amellus* is not used here in its botanical sense. It covers, for horticulturists, a group of similar varieties and hybrids of very different geographical origin including Central Europe, Southern Europe, the East.
The variety 'October Dawn' is upright growing and does not require a stake. Height 20 ins. Diameter of heads 2 ins. Flowering August-October.

37 Aster amellus '*Sonia*'

In a sunny, sheltered position it generally flowers a very long time. Height 24 ins. Diameter of the heads 2¼ ins. Flowering August-October.

38 Aster sedifolius acris nanus

Plant 24 ins. in height. Forms thick trusses. Diameter of the heads 1½-2 ins. Flowering August-October. Give the same spacing as the other asters of the same height, that is allow 2 ft between the plants.

39 Aster amellus
'*Wonder of Stafa*'

Sometimes known as 'Frikartii', this variety requires supporting in unsheltered places. Flowering often commences in July and continues until September. Height of the plant 3 ft. Diameter of the heads 2½ ins.

40 Aster amellus
'*Goblin*'

Height 20 ins. Flowering August-mid-October. Heads of deep cobalt blue; diameter 2¼ ins. To obtain a decorative effect, plant in fairly large groups.

41 Aster ericoides

Perennial. The reduced dimensions of the flowers and the dainty foliage give an impression of lightness. The heads are disposed along the branches which measure 36 ins. Flowers extremely well, and is as suitable as a cut flower as for borders. Frequent transplanting is necessary to avoid cryptogamic diseases. Good varieties: 'Clio', white; 'Golden Spray', yellow; 'Esther', rose-lilac.

42 Aster Novi-belgii
'*Royal Blue*'

All autumn asters gain by being transplanted every two years. They generally endure the frosts. All are suitable for making up bouquets and sheaves. They are also splendid for borders. 'Royal Blue' flowers early (beginning in September) and for a long time. A hardy plant attaining a height of about 5 ft, it is considered the best blue variety. Diameter of the heads 1¼ ins.

43 Aster alpinus superbus

Suitable for rockeries and borders. Flowers extremely well. Diameter of the heads 1½ ins. Flowering May-June. Plant in spring if possible. Height 10 ins. Plant at intervals of 10 ins.

44 Aster Novi-belgii
'*Beechwood Challenger*'

This was the first red variety of *Aster Novi-belgii* to be used in our gardens. The intensity of its colouring has yet to be surpassed. Height 48 ins. Diameter of the head 1½ ins. Flowering September-October.

45 Aster hybridus
'*Pink Lady*'

Hardy. Height 56 ins. Diameter of the heads 1¼-1½ ins. Flowering September-October.

46-50 Astilbe arendsii *hybrids*
(*False Goat's Beard*)

These hybrids are dedicated to Georg Arend, German specialist in astilbes, creator of the best horticultural varieties. They result from the crossings between *Astilbe Davidii* and four east-Asiatic species. The name of meadowsweet is often, but wrongly, attributed to astilbes. The best results are obtained by cultivating in half-shade, in a well aired, warm, yet moist, acid soil. Peat and manure may be used with advantage to enrich the soil. In exposed places astilbes can be covered with dry leaves during the heavy frosts. Excellent for cut flowers, astilbes take their place with clumps of perennial plants surrounding lakes, in front of groups of rhododendrons and azaleas. Spacing varies according to height, in general plant 12 inches or more apart.

46 Astilbe arendsii hybrida

When the rays of the sun touch a humid drop of dew, they seem to fill it with glittering crystals, hence the name of this hybrid might be rock crystal. Height 32-40 ins. Height of the flowering branches, 8 ins. Flowering takes place in July.

47 Astilbe
'Fanal'

Height 16-20 ins. Length of the flowering branches, 6 ins. Flowering July. Lends itself to forcing.

48 Astilbe
'Ceres'

Very elegant. Height 20-24 ins. Length of the flowering stems, 6 ins. Flowering July.

49 Astilbe
'Purple Glory'

A mutation of the rose variety 'Gloria'. Foliage is red-brown in colour. Height 24 ins. Height of the flowering branches 7 ins. Flowering takes place in July.

50 Astilbe
'Queen of Laughter'

One of the oldest varieties, whose colouring has remained unequalled. It seems less exacting than the other varieties over matters of soil. Height 32 ins. Length of the flowering stems 6 ins. Flowering July.

51 Astrantia major *(Masterwort)*

Perennial plant found on the sub-alpine slopes of mountainous regions. One of the oldest garden flowers. Easy to grow, it reaches full development in clay soil in the sun or in half-shade. Resows itself if condition favourable. Height 20-32 ins. Flowering from June to August. It can be used in borders or for growing under trees or shrubs. The flowers last for a long time when cut and are suitable for mixed bouquets.

52-57 Aubrieta *(Purple Rock Cress)*

This genus owes its name to the French botanist, Claude Aubriet, and is a native of the Meditterranean region. It is difficult to imagine any rockery being without *Aubrieta deltoides*, a plant with numerous and brightly coloured flowers. Plant preferably in the autumn. For spring planting, try to retain the soil adhering to the roots. With ten plants to the square yard a beautiful result is obtained after the first year. A sunny aspect is to be preferred. All types of soil are suitable, as long as they are not too dry. Aubrieta puts forth many stems, its new shoots and its flowers appearing at the end of the runners. It has a tendency, after a few years, to lose its foliage in places. This is remedied by cutting away the oldest parts, immediately after flowering and, preferably, quite near the roots. The new shoots are formed rapidly, and flowering the following summer is just as prolific. Flowering from April to the end of May, there are both early and late varieties.

52 Aubrieta deltoides

Flowers early, producing fairly small flowers. It is shown to advantage in the gaps of walls.

53 Aubrieta
'Crimson King'

Large, early flowering variety. The stem are a little soft.

54 Aubrieta
'Dr. Mules'

Semi-early. Large flowers. One of the most hardy varieties.

55 Aubrieta
'Purple Robe'

Semi-dwarf variety, late, with pretty foliage.

56 Aubrieta
'King Waldemar'

Flowers for a month. When planted in a stony soil, the foliage may well be burnt the by sun.

57 Aubrieta

lavender hybrid

Semi-early variety; has large flowers, and fairly soft stems. It can be grown in a lightly shaded place.

58-61 Begonia semperflorens

Native species of Brazil. The word *semperflorens* means 'always flowering', and no more appropriate name could be found. It is useless to try to obtain these plants from outdoor sowings for they must be sown, from January, in a greenhouse and be transplanted several times. They must not be placed in borders or on balconies before all risk of frost has disappeared. It is in the interest of growers to mix peat with the soil to ensure that the plants turn out well. Sun is absolutely necessary; avoid windy positions. Relatively superficial rooting. In a period of drought water regularly before the plants suffer Plant at intervals of 5 ins. When buying plants pay careful attention to the conditions previously experienced by the specimens you are buying. A good point to bear in mind is to make sure that the varieties with red flowers have the brown-red edge to their leaves. Summer begonias are rarely more than 8 ins. in height. The average height of the flower stems is 1 in. This species is particularly suitable for clumps or baskets of at least one square yard. They can be mixed with other plants.

58 Begonia semperflorens

'Red Pearl'

Has very intense colouring. Foliage is dark brown-red. It produces the best effect with plain surroundings. Use it in the garden, either hanging or near a plain wall.

59 Begonia semperflorens

'Prima-Donna'

Particularly suitable for single groups or mixed with other plants. Its plae rose colouring harmonises well with that of the Ageratum and the Sage.

60 Begonia semperflorens

'Tausendschon'

Suitable for many purposes.

61 Begonia semperflorens

'Carpet of Snow'

Useful as a contrast to the other colours.

62-65 Begonia tuberhybrida

These begonias, with large flowers, possess tubers which can be kept in a dormant state from November until April by being put in a cool frost-proof place, packed in peat or sand. In March, put them under frames in pots or boxes of sand and peat. The top part of the tuber should not be completely covered. Soak the soil and place the tubers in the light with a moderate temperature. They should not be transplanted outdoors before the end of the frosts. Harden the plants by leaving the boxes and pots outside in relatively sheltered places. This transplanting should preferably be done in cloudy weather. The tubers can be put directly into the ground, but flowering will then be much later. Tuberous begonias are fragile; they require shelter and half-shade. They like being planted closely together.

62 Begonia multiflora

'Flamboyant'

Multi-flowering begonias have smaller flowers than the other tuberous begonias, but they are less fragile and more prolific in their flowering. 'Flamboyant' attains a height of from 8-10 ins. Diameter of the flowers $1\frac{1}{2}$ ins.

63 Begonia multiflora
'*Frau Helen Harms*'

Taller than the other yellow varieties; a more elegant plant with relatively small flowers which stand up well to the wind. For this reason, it can be planted in flower stands on balconies in non-shaded places. Height 6-8 ins.: diameter ⅜ ins.

64 Begonia
giant flowered tuberous

Height 12-16 ins. Single or double flowers of various colours. There are numerous varieties of tuberous begonias. Among the varieties with rich colours the following groups can be distinguished: single, double, cristata and fimbriata. Double begonias are less suitable for the open ground, because of the very great heaviness of their flowers. Cristata and fimbriata begonias can be regarded as very similar. For making up large groups, single begonias are to be preferred. Tuberous begonias exist in practically every colour, except blue and green. The dimension of the flowers varies between 2-4 ins.

65 Begonia
'*Madame Oscar Lamarck*'

Extremely hardy and flowers well. The tubers can be divided at planting time.

66 Bellis perennis
(*Easter Daisy*)

Horticultural varieties which can be grown, no matter what the soil, have been obtained from the little Easter Daisy. The variety 'Purple Mantle' can be increased by division, which will improve flowering. Flowers from the month of May throughout the summer. Suitable for borders rockeries, surrounding stretches of water, etc. Height 4 ins. Diameter of the heads ⅜ inch.

67 Bellis perennis
double flowered

Normally the Easter Daisy possesses round the circumference of its head, a single row of ligulate flowers, white or rose-coloured. By culture, yellow stamens, making up the centre of the flower, have been replaced by white, rose-coloured or red ligulate florets. The Easter Daisies are then said to be 'with double flowers', an incorrect botanical expression.

A multitude of varieties exist which can be distinguished according to the shape of the ligules: the variety ligulosa has plain, flat ligules; fistulosa, trumpet-shaped, tuberous ligules. Reproduces by seed, although the seed does not assure the perfect transmission of the colours. Sow in June. Transplant at the end of summer and put in place in the following spring. On the oldest plants, the heads become smaller and more simple with less numerous ligules. It is advisable to cultivate Bellis like a biennial plant. This variety is suitable for baskets and rockeries. Flowers almost all the summer but the heads are more beautiful in spring and at the beginning of summer. Height 4-6 ins. Diameter of the heads 1-2 ins.

68 Bergenia cordifolia *purpurea*
(*Large-leaved Saxifrage*)

Native of the mountain regions of the East and Asia. This is one of the rare perennials which, having large leaves, keeps them in winter. It prefers half-shade and requires a rich and, if possible, humid soil. Flowers in very early spring. Length of the floral stalks 8 ins. Diameter of the leaves 4-6 ins. Very decorative, even in the absence of flowers. To be at its best, it requires a suitable site, for example, around ponds or lakes. The plants can be mixed with ferns or azaleas; they are very suitable also for rockeries or when first planting a grove. In the middle of April cut off the winter foliage to facilitate the shoots of the new leaves.

69 Briza maxima
(Pearl Grass)

Grass-like plant with big epillets, native of the Mediterranean countries, close relative of the modest *Briza media*, frequenter of lawns. An annual species which is sown directly in its place in a warm, sunny position. Ensure that it has sufficient light. Plant at intervals of 4 ins. The heads appear in July. Length of the epillets ½-1¾ ins. It can be preserved dry for winter decoration.

70 Butomus umbellatus
(Flowering Rush)

A marsh plant, perennial and a native. Plant around marshy basins and on the edge of lakes. Flowers June until August. Height 40 ins.

71 Calceolaria integrifolia

A native of Chile, this shrub produces many branches. Its dwarf variety is particularly valued. Propagate in a greenhouse by cuttings or from seed. Only plant outdoors when all risk of frost has gone; it is very sensitive to variations in temperature. Flowers abundantly from June-July to October. Produces a splendid effect when mixed with other plants with brightly coloured flowers.

72 Calceolaria polyrrhiza
(Slipper Flower)

Native of Patagonia. Perennial. Suitable for rockeries. Carpet-like in form. The flowering stems have a height of 4 ins. Flowering June to August. It should be partly shaded but likes a sunny aspect. Protect in winter.

73 Calendula officinalis
'Balls Orange' (Pot Marigold)

Orange double garden marigold. Ancient medicinal plant, hence its name of *officinalis*. The species, a native of the South of Europe, has single heads. It is not just by chance that the marigold has become one of our popular summer plants: it has few essential requirements and produces many heads. Flowering is from June to the end of the autumn. It sows itself on the same spot each year, and is happy in firm soil with some warmth from the sun. It should be planted at distances of 12 ins. It has a number of uses and goes as well with annual plants as with perennials. A good plant for cut flowers.

74 Calendula officinalis
'Balls Gold'

Golden double garden marigold. Like the previous plants, flowers excellently in summer, and reaches the same height 12-16 ins.
Diameter of the heads 1½ ins.

75-78 Callistephus chinensis
(Starwort or China Aster)

The two words which describe this species mean: the first, pretty wreath (coronet, crown), the other indicates the country where it was produced. Since its introduction, ceaseless attempts have been made to perfect this plant and multiply the varieties. China asters are very good flowers to cut and last a fairly long time in water. They are also suitable for making good plants in borders and rockeries. It is preferable to sow under glass and only to put into place when the plants are fairly well developed. A well-prepared soil is needed and a sunny position. For the tall varieties, space at intervals of 12 ins.; 8 ins. for the semi-dwarf varieties and 4 ins. for the dwarf ones.

In general, flowering commences in August for the early species, in September for the late species.

75 Callistephus chinensis
China Aster

Height 24 ins. approximately. Fairly early flowering. Like the varieties mentioned below, the flowers are available in many colours.

76 Callistephus chinensis
'Marguerite' Aster

Lovers of single China asters will choose this variety. Height 20-24 ins. Early flowering.

77 Callistephus chinensis
'Ostrich Plume' Aster

A variety of high quality greatly treasured for making up fine bunches and bouquets with long stems. Semi-early flowering, attains a height of 24 ins.

78 Callistephus chinensis
'Lilliput' Aster

A short plant (12 ins.) and with heads of good size (diameter 1¼ ins.). Semi-early. It is suitable for borders and clumps, and excellent also as a pot plant.

79 Calla palustris
(Marsh Calla or Bog Arum)

Grows freely beside lakes and in marshes. Sometimes difficult to acclimatise in ponds or artificial pieces of water because of the water being too alkaline. In such cases add sulphate of ammonium $(NH_4)_2SO_4$. When planting, attach to a support sunk in the soil until the roots have formed. Flowering June-August. Diameter of the flower 1¼ ins. The flower is composed of an axis bearing the flowers surrounded by a white spathe.

80 Calla palustris
double

Variety with double flowers thicker and shorter than **Caltha palustris**, which has single flowers. Seems to require less moisture; plant closer together.

81 Caltha palustris *single*
(Marsh Marigold or Kingcup)

The Greek word Calathos means a basket and the name Caltha thus calls to mind the basket-shape of the corolla. It inhabits marshy places throughout almost the whole of Britain, and should only be cultivated in such places as the edges of lakes, streams, springs and damp slopes. Flowering from April to the end of June. Height 16 ins. Diameter of the flowers 1¾ ins. Six plants can be grown in a square yard.

82-84 Canna indica *(Indian Shot)*

All our cultivated cannas are the result of hybridising. In winter, keep the rhizomes sheltered from light, frost and damp. Start into growth early in March, and expose to the light as soon as the first shoots appear. Put in flowering places at the end of May, after the frosts. Cannas are to be recommended for the forming of clumps; they can be set out in groups near ponds and lakes. They do not go well with other perennial plants.

82 Canna indica
Indian hybrids

Leaves 16 ins. long, 6 ins. wide of a dark bluish-green colour, with violaceus secondary ribs and green primary ribs edged with violet. Length of the flowering stalk 10 ins. Flowers 3 ins. in diameter. Height of the plant 36 ins.

83 Canna indica
Shot or speckled canna

Height of the plant 36 ins. Leaves from

14-18 ins. in length and 7½ ins. wide, bright green in colour with greeny-yellow ribs. Flowers are 4 ins. in diameter.

84 Canna indica hybrida
pale pink Indian hybrid

Height of the plant 36 ins. Leaves 16 ins. long and 9½ ins. wide. Height of flower stalk 8 ins. Diameter of the flower 4 ins.

85-90 Campanula *(Bellflower)*

The latin name *Campanula* refers to the bell-shape of the corollas. Many species are known to grow wild in Britain, almost all with blue flowers, a few being yellowish or white. They live in very varied positions, both on low and high ground; some on limy soils, others on flinty ground, and in woods and meadows.

85 Campanula carpatica

Forms thick clumps 12 ins. in height. Diameter of the flowers 1½ ins. Flowering June to September. Perennial. They are suitable for borders and rockeries, and can be planted either in the spring or autumn. Plant at intervals of 8 ins. Among the best varieties are: *alba*, white; Isabelle, large bright blue; Wilsonii, large deep blue.

86 Campanula glomerata dahurica

A cultivated form of *Campanula glomerata*. Height 20-24 ins. Flowering June to August. It is best suited to a limy soil and a sunny position. A good flower for cutting. Excellent for perennial borders.

87 Campanula media
(Canterbury Bell)

This plant grows wild on hills and in mountainous districts. Biennial. A very beautiful plant for cut flowers and pots. Seed should be sown in June; trans-planting and putting into place in September. Flowering May-July of the following year. Height: 32 ins. It forms little bells 3 ins. long and 1½ ins. wide. It exists in numerous colours: white, rose and through to the deepest blues. Single or semi-double. Requires a good firm soil, a sunny aspect and some shade. Protect the plants during winter.

88 Campanula persicifolia

The campanula with peach leaves can be found in the hilly woods of almost the whole of Europe. The leaves form clusters of a bright green; the flowers rise elegantly on their slender stalks. Height 32-40 ins. Diameter of the flowers 1¾ ins. Likes the sun. It is most suitable for perennial borders.

A white semi-double variety that is worth cultivating, is *Moerheimii*.

89 Campanula portenschlagiana

Native of Dalmatia. The best of the species, without a doubt, for walls and rockeries. In a sunny or half-shaded position, it soon forms compact trusses which flower without ceasing from June to August. Height 5-6 ins.

90 Campanula pusilla
(Dwarf Campanula)

Plant growing in the rocky parts of the following mountains: Pyrenees (Pyrenean mountains), Alpes, Vosges, Jura and Carpathian mountains. It does well in half-shade in light limy soils. Flowering June-August. Height 2-8 ins.

C. pulla is a similar dwarf species.

91 Centaurea cyanus
(Blue Cornflower)

Cultivated chiefly as a cut flower. Sows itself in the same place. By sowing every fortnight, from March to August, flowers can be obtained throughout the summer. The last seeds winter and flower from the month of May. Cornflowers come in all colours, but the blue ones remain the most beautiful.

92 Centaurea montana *rose*

This plant only differs from the variety following by its colouring.

93 Centaurea montana
blue, rose centre

This plant is a flower of the fields, woods and mountain sides. It is of value because of its continuous flowering from May to July. It is good for cutting and useful for bright flower-beds and large rock gardens. Fresh flowering in autumn. It multiplies rapidly. Its height is 20 ins.

94 Centranthus ruber *(Valerian)*
var. 'Coccineus'

Though a native of Southern Europe, this plant thrives everywhere. It is a beautiful subject for flower-beds. The flowering can be prolonged, if the first flower stems are cut off in July. It has the advantage also of having no special requirements as regards soil and moisture.

95 Cerastium biebersteinii
Snow-in-Summer

This flower was originally from the Crimea; it grows vigorously and is liable to become invasive. It is just the type to serve for a kind of 'flower carpet' and is admirably suited to fill up blank spaces in rock gardens. It flowers for a fortnight in July. Height is from 8 to 12 ins. It puts up with the damp of winter, with difficulty, but has no other special need beyond attention to that point.

96 Cheiranthus cheiri
(Wallflower)

The strange name of Cheiranthus is formed from Kheiri, the Arabian name of Wallflower, and Anthos the Greek name for flower. This flower, originally from Orient, has become naturalised and grown long since in Britain and elsewhere. Though by nature perennial it is usually grown as a biennial. It is best sown in May and June and spaced out in July. The flowering is then in the following spring. The double form can be planted in pots and will flower in winter. They are in several shades of yellow, red, and brown. Their height is about 20 ins.

97 Cheiranthus allionii

This kind of plant develops more rapidly than the preceeding one. By being sown under glass in the spring, it will flower like an annual in July-August. If sown later, it will become biennial. It is a good flower for beds and borders.

98 Chiastophyllum oppositifolium

Very suitable for rockeries and dry walls. It needs a dry situation especially during winter. It flowers in June and July. The many bunches of flowers about 3 ins. long, remind one of the cytisus, and are particularly decorative. It prefers half-shade. Plant at the rate of 25 to the square yard. It is often known as Cotyledon.

99-106 Chrysanthemums

The species *C. indicum* and *C. morifolium* are probably natives of China and Japan, while *C. koreanum* comes from Korea. Chrysanthemums are grown in large quantities, and innumerable varieties exist. Those mentioned are among the best adapted for gardens. It is preferable to dig up after flowering and to put them in shelter from the winter frosts. They should be watched carefully so as not to be allowed to dry up. In the spring, generally in March, new shoots appear. The plants should then be placed in the light and the shoots cut when they are about 3 ins. long. These cuttings are placed under frames in sand. When they have taken root they are transplanted and put into place. If only a few plants are wanted, the simplest thing is to divide the clumps and to plant them directly. Chrysanthemums prefer to grow in really good soils. They are big 'consumers', and it is essential to supply them with rich and nourishing soil, if one wishes to obtain fine flowers and good growth. When the chrysanthemums are fairly strong the tops are nipped off, to encourage bushiness. Water in dry weather. Generally speaking, they are only placed in vases when they are in full bloom. The chrysanthemum is undoubtedly one of the best flowers for cutting in the autumn.

99 Chrysanthemum indicum
'*Gold Dust*'

Flowering September-October. Very floriferous and very agreeable. Height 20 ins. Diameter 2½ ins.

100 Chrysanthemum indicum
'*Anastasia*'

Flowers from the end of August. Height 16 ins. Diameter of the heads 2 ins.

101 Chrysanthemum Korean hybrid
'*Apollo*'

Very hardy. Flowers October-November. Height 32 ins. Diameter of head 2¼ ins.

102 Chrysanthemum Korean hybrid
'*Hebe*'

One of the strongest. Flowers September-October. Height 32 ins. Diameter of head 2¾ ins.

103 Chrysanthemum indicum
'*Gobelin*'

Excellent hybrid. Flowers September-October. Height 24 ins. Diameter of head 2⅝ ins.

104 Chrysanthemum indicum
'*September Gold*'

Keeps its colour well. Flowers September-October. Height 20 ins. Diameter of flowers 2½ ins.

105 Chrysanthemum indicum
'*Phoenix*'

A good flower for cutting. Grows very upright Flowers September-October. Height 32 ins. Diameter of flowers 2⅝ ins.

106 Chrysanthemum indicum
'*Madame Marie Masse*'

One of the best chrysanthemums and the most frequently grown. Flowers September-October. Height 24 ins. Diameter of flowers 2¾ ins.

107-110 Chrysanthemum coccineum

This species, which comes originally from the Caucasus and Armenia, is one of our strongest plants for flower-beds and for cutting. Plants should be spaced 20 ins. apart, and they thrive in all firm soils. They favour sunny positions.

107 Chrysanthemum coccineum
(*Pyrethrum*)
'*Eileen May Robinson*'

Hardy. Height 32 ins. Very large flowers during May-July-August. Useful for many purposes.

108 Chrysanthemum coccineum
(*Pyrethrum*)
'*James Kelway*'

Of fine appearance in flower-beds. Height 24 ins. Flowers May-June.

109 Chrysanthemum maximum
'Universal' (Shasta Daisy)

Comes originally from the Pyrenees. Some horticultural varieties surpass it in height and in beauty. Indispensable for flower-beds; likes a sunny position. A very fine flower for cutting. Height 28 ins. Diameter of flowers 3 ins.

110 Chrysanthemum coccineum
(Pyrethrum)
'Queen Mary'

Though less flourishing than the preceeding plant, it can be mixed with other livelier flowers. Height 16 ins. Diameter of flowers 2¾ ins. Flowers in May-July. Among the double-flowered types are 'Queen Mary' (pink) and 'Lord Roseberry' (red).

111 Chrysanthemum segetum
'Eldorado'

Annual, very flourishing and easily grown. Grows from self-sown seed immediately after the frosts. Thin out to 10 ins. Height 20-28 ins. Flowers July-August. Good for cutting. The garden varieties have much larger flowers than the wild plant and the colouring varies from yellow to white-cream.

112 Chrysanthemum carinatum tricolor

Comes originally from North Africa. Annual. It, grown like the preceding variety. Flowers without stopping from July-October. Height 20-28 ins. Suitable for the flower-bed and for cutting. Like all annual Chrysanthemums, it needs a sunny position. Available in several colours including white, lilac, yellow and red.

113 Chrysanthemum frutescens

A native of the Canaries and perennial, but unable to endure temperatures of below 3° centigrade. May be grown from seed. Plants to be placed in the open ground after the frosts. It can be increased by cuttings from the root which has passed the winter under glass. Replant, nip off surplus shoots and accustom gradually to open air conditions before definitely placing outdoors. It seldom grows higher than 16 ins. Flowers from the beginning of summer until the frosts.

114 Chrysanthemum coronarium

A native of Southern Europe. White or yellow petals, but the discus of the flower is always yellow. There are also double flowers. For cultivation and uses, see 111 and 112.

115 Clarkia elegans double mixed

This plant, a native of California, has single flowers, but double flowers appear in the cultivated forms. Annual. Sow directly in flowering position and thin out to 10 ins. apart. Sunny position and dry. Height 20-32 ins. Highly decorative when used in flower-beds and borders (in groups). The flower stems, once cut, only keep if the leaves are stripped off.

116 Cimicifuga dahurica (Bugbane)
'Silver Spike'

Plant is perennial and robust, coming from Central Asia. It prefers damp soil and a semi-shady background. It is grown generally in flower-beds or with bergenia, corydalis, hepatica etc. Flowers July-September. Good for cutting. It has a strong but disagreeable odour.

117 Cimicifuga racemosa

Comes originally from North America. Taller than the preceeding; also more beautiful. Flowering, cultivation and use are the same as C. dahurica.

118 Cobaea scandens
(Canterbury Bell Vine)

The genus Cobaea was named after the

Spanish Jesuit and botanist Cobo. *C. Scandens* comes from Mexico. It is a perennial but generally treated as an annual, for it cannot stand the frosts. It must be sown in greenhouses and transplanted into fair sized pots as soon as the tufts appear, and be supported. Considered an excellent creeper and useful for the decoration of balconies, verandahs etc. It reaches 8-10 ft high during the summer. Well-manured soil and a sunny position suit it.

119 Colchicum autumnale
(Meadow Saffron or Autumn Crocus)

The mauve cups of the colchicum appear from late August until October; the leaves appear in the following spring. Plant up to 3 ins. deep. From the colchicum a poisonous substance, colchicine, is extracted which is used by geneticians to create modifications in plant cells.

120 Convallaria majalis
(Lily of the Valley)

Long-rooted perennial plant, it grows in many conditions. The leaves appear in March and April and the flowering stems in April-May. It is appreciated particularly for its elegance and for the delicious perfume of its white bell-flowers. Plant in autumn, preferably in large groups.

121 Coreopsis tinctoria *(Tickseed)*

The elegant annual coreopsis. A native of North America. It should be sown in April. Flowers June to September. Height 20-32 ins., but only 14 ins. in the dwarf types. Likes light soil and plenty of sun. Excellent for flower-beds, and also for cutting. There are many varieties.

122 Coreopsis verticillata grandiflora

This plant comes originally from North America, but becomes rapidly acclimatised quite far towards the North. Perennial. Dislikes the damp. The plants are raised from seeds sown in March in sunny flower-beds and big rockeries. Good for cutting. Flowers July-September; diameter 18 ins.

123 Cosmos bipinnatus
(Purple Mexican Aster)

This plant, originally from Mexico, is related to the dahlia. It cannot be kept indefinitely in the garden, but only until the beginning of the frosts. Sow directly in the ground or in boxes. Height 2½-4 feet. Diameter of the flowers 2 ins. Flowers July-October. Likes a sunny position, and has few requirements. Good for beds or cutting.

124 Corydalis lutea
(Yellow Fumitory)

This often remains green nearly all the year round. Height 9 ins. Flowers from April to the frosts. It has few requirements and is frequently found on rockeries and on old wallsides. It sows itself freely.

125 Crocus aureus

This should be planted and used as other spring crocuses. Plant the bulbs in September-October at a depth of 3 ins. in moist but well drained soil. The flowering depends on the weather conditions, but generally takes place in March-April. Height 3-3½ ins. Most suitable for lawns, flower beds and rockeries.

126 Crocus speciosus

This elegant crocus is originally from the Caucasus. The bulbs should be planted in July. Flowers September-October. Leaves develop after flowers.

127 Crocus vernus

There are a great number of this type,

which flowers even in February, but more often in March; the flowers follow one another for about a month. Looks well in groups or separate beds, has few requirements but prefers rich and fresh soil.

128 Cyclamen neapolitanum

This plant becomes rapidly established in shady parks and lawns. The leaves are of varied shapes and generally decked with a silvery edge. Flowers in September-October and the leaves continue all the winter. The tubers should be planted in shallow ground, little more than half an inch deep. Prefers, above all, shade or semi-shade in acid and light soil.

129 Cypripedium calceolus
(Lady's Slipper)

This orchid, which lives in woods or hilly pastures, prefers very moist and neutral soil; it is sufficient if the depth is only 3 or 4 ins. for the roots go no deeper. Leave the roots near the surface. It should not be dug up unnecessarily. Likes a shady or semi-shady aspect. Flowers May-June. This 'Lady's Slipper', which is in some danger of extinction, should be protected. There is another orchid still more beautiful and not much more difficult to grow, the Queen of Cypripedium.

130-171 Dahlias

The word dahlia recalls the name of a Swedish botanist, a follower of Linnaeus, Doctor Andreas Dahl. The first dahlia was brought from Mexico to Europe about 1784. Later a dozen types were created by crossing these plants, and many types are now to be obtained. Propagation is effected either by cuttings, or by the division of the tubers. The planting of the entire tubers produces only small flowers. A week before planting (sometime during May)

the tubers should be separated, and should be watered daily to encourage growth. They should be planted below 3 ins. of soil, and at distances more or less approximative to the type of plant. Stakes should be put in at the same time so that as they grow they can be supported solidly. At the time of flowering, label carefully, so that the names remain visible the following spring.

After flowering, cut the stems at about 5 ins. above the tubers. The first frosts blacken stalks and leaves; the tubers should be allowed to remain in the earth for some days longer, then dug up carefully. During the winter, keep the tubers sheltered from frost in dry sand or in peat, and avoid dampness. Dahlias prefer good garden soil and a sheltered and sunny position. Artificial fertilizers should not be over-employed. Flowering begins in late June and continues till the frosts. Dahlias can be used for many purposes. They should be placed according to their size and in the most varied places. Excellent as a garden flower. It is possible to recognise amongst the dahlias a great variety of types, with flowers of many sizes, colours and shapes.

From this it is easy to judge that the development of the present species represents only a small part of the variety of plants that could be realised by hybridisation. Dahlias are grouped according to their form and shape of flower: including Decorative Dahlias, mainly flat-petalled, varying between the water lily type and ball type of flower; and Cactus Dahlias, and hybrids from the Cactus, with petals generally pointed and twined.

130 Dahlia
'Italia'

This is very attractive and grows nearly 5 ft in height, with flowers 8 ins. in diameter.

131 Dahlia

single mixed

This is a dainty type of dahlia. It exists in several different colours, and is very suitable for flower-beds.

132 Dahlia

'Oslo'

Another very attractive dahlia. Height 5 ft; diameter of the flowers 5½ ins.

133 Dahlia

'Helly Boudewyn'

The height of this plant is 4½ ft and the diameter of flowers 4 ins.

134 Dahlia

'Thor'

A dahlia of the water lily type. Its height is 3½ ft, with its flowers nearly 3 ins. in diameter. This is a good flower for cutting.

135 Dahlia

'General Carl Moltke'

This plant is a dahlia of ball form, 3 ft high, with the diameter of flowers nearly 3 ins. It is suitable for flower-beds, and good for cutting.

136 Dahlia

'Golden Leader'

This is most attractive. The height is 3½ ft with the diameter of the flowers 5 ins.

137 Dahlia

'Riante'

This dahlia is a water-lily type of a height of 2¾ ft with the diameter of flowers 3 ins. Fine for flower-beds and cutting.

138 Dahlia

'Bacchus'

This water-lily type is of a height of 3½ ft with flowers of over 3 ins.

139 Dahlia

'Gerrie Hoek'

This is a decorative with a diameter of 4 ins. for its flowers. Good for flower-beds.

140 Dahlia

'Arc de Triomphe'

This plant is a medium decorative and of a height of 3½ ft. The diameter of its flowers is 5 ins.

141 Dahlia

'Troef'

This plant is very striking. Its height is 3 ft and the diameter of its flowers is 4 ins. Sometimes listed as 'Truth'.

142 Dahlia

'Ballego's Glory'

This water-lily type of plant is 3¾ ft in height and its flowers over 3 ins. in diameter. It is a flower for cutting as well as for garden decoration.

143 Dahlia

'Vermilion Brilliant'

This is a magnificent plant of a height of 4 ft with the flowers 3 ins. in diameter.

144 Dahlia

'Andries Pink'

This plant grows nearly 3 ft high, its flowers being 3 ins. in diameter.

145 Dahlia

'Ahoy'

A decorative plant of 3 ft in height, with flowers 4½ ins. in diameter.

146 Dahlia

'Therose'

A water-lily type of plant, this dahlia is 3½ ft in height, its flowers being up to 3 ins. across.

147 Dahlia
'Duindigt'

This cactus type of dahlia grows to a height of 4¾ ft, and has flowers with a diameter of 6¼ ins.

148 Dahlia
'Brandaris'

This hybrid type of the cactus dahlia has a height of 5 ft and the diameter of its flowers is 5 ins.

149 Dahlia
'Yellow Special'

This water-lily type of dahlia grows about 3 ft high, and its flowers are 6 ins. in diameter. Place two or three plants to the square yard.

150 Dahlia
'Good Morning'

This cactus type grows to a height of 4½ ft and its flowers have a diameter of 4¾ ins.

151 Dahlia
'Fine Anniversary'

This is another cactus variety with a height of 4½ ft and flowers 5 ins. in diameter.

152 Dahlia
'Silvoretta'.

Yet another cactus variety, 4 ft in height with flowers 5½ ins. in diameter.

153 Dahlia
'Pin Up'

Another cactus variety with a height of 3½ ft and the diameter of its flowers 5¼ ins.

154 Dahlia
'White Superior'

This is also a cactus dahlia of a height of 5½ ft high. The diameter of its flowers is nearly 6 ins.

155 Dahlia
'Bronze Elsie Crellin'

This plant is a water-lily type, of a height of 4 and its flowers are 5 ins. in diameter.

156 Dahlia
'Elsie Crellin'

Also a water-lily type of plant, of a height of 4½ ft and with flowers 5 ins. in diameter.

157 Dahlia
'Baby Rose'

A decorative plant of a height of 4½ ft with flowers over 5 ins. in diameter. It is suitable for group planting and the flowers are excellent for cutting.

158 Dahlia
'Freda'

This water-lily type of plant is of a height of 4½ ft and its flowers have a diameter of 4½ ins.

159 Dahlia
'Goldelse'

Another water-lily type. Its height is 4 ft, the diameter of its flowers 4 ins.

160 Dahlia
'A propos'

A pompon type. Its height is 4 ft and the flowers are 1¾ ins. in diameter.

161 Dahlia
'Heloise'

Another pompon. Its height is 4½ ft, and the diameter of its flowers 2 ins.

162 Dahlia
'Nerissa'

Also a pompon. Height 3¾ feet. The flowers have a diameter of 1¾ ins.

163 Dahlia
'Kochelse'

A pompon. Its height is 3¾ feet and its flowers 2¼ ins. in diameter.

164 Dahlia
    'Pinnochio'

One more pompon. Its height is 5 ft with flowers 1¼ ins. diameter. This is especially a flower for cutting.

165 Dahlia
    'Zonnegoud'

A pompon. Its height is 4¾ ft and its flowers 2¼ ins. diameter.

166 Dahlia
    'Sonia'

A pompon plant, 4¾ ft high, with a diameter of 2 ins. for its flowers.

167 Dahlia
    'Symphonia'

A semi-double type of 4¾ ft in height The diameter of its flowers is 3¾ ins. The foliage is very dark in colour.

168 Dahlia
    'Snow Princess'

A plant of the single type. Its height is 4¾ ft and its flowers have a diameter of 3¾ ins.

169 Dahlia
    'Light of the Moon'

Collarette type. Its height is only 3¼ ft and the diameter of its flowers 4¾ ins.

170 Dahlia
    'Colorit'

Better known as a 'Collarette dahlia. Its height is 4¾ ft and its flowers have a width of 3¾ ins.

171 Dahlia
    'La Cierva'

A collarette type. Its height is 4½ ft, and the flowers are 4¼ ins. diameter.

172-178 Delphiniums

The perennial larkspur can be counted among the most beautiful plants for the flower bed. Many of the varieties are very tall, and owing to their height need early supporting. They are not exacting plants in so far as the soil is concerned, though rich ground is preferable, and they should be kept moist, both before and during the flowering, which takes place from May-July. They like plenty of sun, and it is wise to protect them from severe frosts. Many of this type are reproduced from seed. To keep the plants true to type, the perennials must be increased by cutting or by divisions.

172 Delphinium
    'Constance'

This particular larkspur is strong and upright growing. It is rather precocious in its growth and well flowered. Diameter of the flowers is 2½ ins. and the height of the plant 5 ft. It is very suitable for flower beds and for cutting.

173 Delphinium
    'Lamartine'

Early and strong. This plant continues growth after flowering, if cut when the 'spikes' finish. Its height is from 3-6 ft and the length of its flowering branches is 12-14 ins.

174 Delphinium
    'Mrs. Thomson'

Semi-precocious and of a dainty type. Its flowering branches are 12-18 ins. long.

175 Delphinium
    Pacific Giant Strain

A new type which has been obtained from the U.S.A. by cross-fertilisation. It has a stalk of strong diameter, and big flowers both single and double, 6-9 ins. in diameter. The height of this plant is from 4½-7 ft. It gives the best results if sown early and grown as an annual or biennial. If this plant is kept more than 2 years, it is apt to lose its characteristics.

176 Delphinium ruysii
'Pink Sensation'

Strong and hardy. The height of this plant is 3 ft and its flowering branches are 12 ins. long. It should be noted that this larkspur seems more floriferous than all others.

177 Delphinium nudicaule

A perennial, originally from California, it needs a well drained soil. It may be grown on rockeries and in the foreground of flower beds of perennials. Its height is 1 ft and its flowering time from May-July.

178 Delphinium *'Persimmon'*

Suitable for the background of beds of perennials. Its height is 5 ft and it has long flowering branches. The diameter of the flowers is 1¾ ins.

179 Dianthus barbatus
(Sweet William)

Really a perennial, though treated generally as biennial. It loses its qualities with time. It should be sown in May, planted out between August and October, and it flowers the following summer from late May till August. Its height is 16 ins. and its colour range is very wide. It is suitable for the borders of flower beds and is a good subject for cutting.

180 Dianthus caryophyllus
(Carnation)

Known also as 'Florists Pink', this is a perennial, though often grown as a biennial. It should be sown in April and May and transplanted. It should be placed early the following spring in a sandy loam which is well drained, with a good aspect. Its flowering is in June-July, and its height from 16-24 ins. Suitable for flower beds and for cutting. It is the type which comes the nearest to the large flowered carnation. It has

numerous varieties with double flowers and very numerous tints of red, white, and pink.

181 Dianthus plumarius *(Pink)*
'Duchess of Fife'

A dainty pink. This delicate plant is originally from South-eastern Europe. All the later varieties are prettier and more ready to flower than the original. It is undoubtedly happiest in a sunny position. It grows quite well on sandy or pebbly ground, preferably fairly rich. It stands the winter well, if protected. It flowers from end of May into July. The floral stems rise to 12 ins. and it is suitable for borders and rockeries. It is very scented and suitable for bouquets.

182 Dianthus caryophyllus
'Countess Knuth'

This plant also has the advantage of being able to withstand the rigours of winter, if not too severe. It is increased by cuttings and by layering. Its flowering is in June-July, and it is extremely floriferous. The height is 14 ins. and it is particularly elegant in flower beds. These pinks are beautiful flowers for cutting.

183 Dianthus plumarius
'Diamant'

A dainty plant. This is a fine garden flower known as both 'Diamant' and 'Diamond', and used similarly to No. 181. It is excellent for cutting and flowers during June and July, growing about 12 ins. high.

184 Dicentra spectabilis

Though originally from China and Japan, this is long since a garden flower of Britain. It flowers from May to June, and its height is 2 ft. It favours a rather shaded position and flowers well under tall trees. If it is intended to be grown in flower beds it should be placed behind plants of lesser height but autumnal flowering, for the leaves of *Dicentra* fade very early. These flowers are very decorative and lasting for fine bouquets.

185 Dimorphotheca aurantiaca
(*Star of the Veldt*)

Though originally from Africa, there are now numerous garden varieties with flowers of yellow, salmon, apricot and white. A warm and sunny position is necessary for this plant. It is annual and flowers from June-August. It should be sown directly in its flower-bed, and be thinned out 6-9 ins. apart.

186 Digitalis purpurea *(Foxglove)*

It takes its name from the Latin word for finger (*digitus*) and is a medicinal plant much used for certain cardiac medicines. It is a good plant for the flower bed, and easy to satisfy as regards soils and situation. It reproduces in abundance. The plants from self-sown seeds are usually the finest. The flowering is from June-August, and the height 2 to 5 ft.

187 Dodecatheon meadia
(*Shooting Star or American Cowslip*)

Flowers in May and is 10 ins. high. It has the advantage of growing either in full sunlight or in the shade. It favours, however, a moderate amount of shade in a moist soil. It looks well in rockeries and in fairly large groupings.

188 Doronicum *(Leopard's Bane)*
'Mrs. Mason'

Comes from the Caucasus, but has long since come to be counted among one of our most interesting and easily grown perennials. It can be grown practically anywhere, and flowers from late March to May. Its height is 26 ins. and the diameter of its flowers 2½ ins.

An excellent plant; suitable for rockeries and flower beds, and for cutting.

189 Dryas octopetala
(*Mountain Avens*)

Grows very freely on the grassy slopes and rockeries of the hilly districts of Europe. This herbaceous plant with its flat, woody stems, is very suitable for sunny rockeries and needs plenty of space. The date of its flowering varies somewhat, according to the district and the situation, from May-July. The leaves continue all through the winter and in snowy weather they often take on a beautiful rusty tint which is generally very much liked. The height of these plants is 6 ins. and they appear very hardy.

190 Echinops ritro
(*Globe Thistle*)

This plant grows wild in some parts. It is a perennial, which can be grown either on lawns or in flower beds. The flower heads can be preserved throughout the winter by drying. For this, the flowering stems should be cut prematurely before the opening of the flowers, in order to conserve their metallic lustre. Flowering is from July-September. They prefer dry ground and plenty of sun.

191 Epimedium grandiflorum
(*Barrenwort*)

Of Japanese origin and a perennial. This plant likes the shade and is suitable for rockeries, walls and shrubberies. The leaves have a slightly leathery texture and continue through all the winter. The flowering is April-May and the height 8-9 ins.

192 Eranthis hiemalis
(*Winter Aconite*)

Takes its name from Greece whence it comes. It also grows wild in other parts of Europe. Flowering is from February onwards. The tubers should be planted from June to October, at 2 ins. deep and 4 ins. apart. It is better to choose the places where this Greek plant can do its own seeding in shrubberies, rockeries etc. Its height is 4 ins.

193 Eremurus bungei
(Foxtail Lily)

This plant, known also as 'The Lily of the Steppes', comes originally from Persia, and is undoubtedly by its resemblance to the hyacinth and its tall stature, among the most remarkable of our garden perennials. It grows better in light, dampish soil, and prefers a very sunny aspect. It comes through the winter without difficulty, even in Northern Europe, but suffers from excessive damp. It is therefore preferable to cover the plants sufficiently during rough weather. If the situation is damp, the roots should be dug up and kept all the winter in the cellar. They may be re-planted in the garden in the spring. The holes in the ground should be dug fairly deep, with a layer of gravel placed at the bottom, the roots should then be well spread out, and covered with 4-5 ins. of soil. Flowering is from May-July, and height 5-8 ft. A fine plant for cutting.

194 Eremurus robustus

'Cleopatra's Distaff', as it has been named so poetically, comes from Turkestan, and is the best known of the eremurus species. It is taller than the previous variety (193) and attains a height of from 7½-9 ft, while the length of the floral stem is from 3-4½ ft, the diameter of each flower being 2½ ins. It flowers in June and July, and needs protection from wind. The same measures should be adopted for its cultivation as for No. 193 The eremurus in general should be placed where they show to advantage. They are suitable in front of shady bushes, or even pines and fir trees.

195-198 Erigerons *(Fleabane)*

This large family of *Compositae* contains more than 350 species, both annual and perennial. They grow throughout the world, but especially in North America. A certain number of the species are now cultivated, and by hybridization have given numerous garden type varieties. The following are perennials. They are easy to grow, strong and very floriferous. They should be planted in autumn or in the spring, in any soil, in full sun or semishade. They stand the climate right up to Northern Europe, but should be placed in beds of perennials, for example with asters *(amellus)*. They should have supports, as their stems are rather fragile.

195 Erigeron speciosum
'*Wupperthal*'

Height 2½ ft. This plant flowers abundantly from July to October. One of the best for flower beds.

196 Erigeron hybridum
'*Quakeress*'

Grows to a height of 2 ft. The leaves are smooth and of a fresh green appearance. The diameter of the flowers is 1¾ ins., and they appear in June-July, often with a second season in September. This plant is highly suitable for flower beds and for cutting.

197 Erigeron hybridum
'*Summer Snow*'

Height 26 ins. It flowers late, during August and September. Its petals are pure white. They are fairly rigid, and can do without supports as a rule.

198 Erigeron speciosum mesa-grande

This well-known flower is 3 ft in height, and is strong and erect. Its flowers are abundant and come in June and July. The diameter of the flowers is 1¾ ins. This is excellent for cutting.

199 Eryngium hybridum
(Sea Holly)

It is happiest in the light soils, and flowers in July-August. Height 4 ft. It should be grown with other perennials.

200 Erythronium dens-canis
(Dog's Tooth Violet)

This pretty flower takes its name from its delicate frilled petals. It grows wild in Central and Southern Europe, especially in mountainous districts. The tubers should be planted in September, 4 ins. deep, and it is preferable to plant them in groups so as to form clumps. They are especially suitable for rockeries, and lawn sides, and look well growing under trees. They should be protected during severe weather. They attain a height of 4-6 ins. The leaves are well veined, and they flower from March-May. Colouring of the flowers varies from white to reddish-violet.

201 Eschscholtzia californica
(Californian Poppy)

This plant originates in the West of North America, as its name indicates. It is well-known here as a good annual. It is easily self-sown, but it is better to destroy the self-sown plants, for the size of their flowers is much smaller. The seeds should be sown where they are to flower, in an open position and good soil. They flower from June to August, and are from 12-20 ins. high, Suitable for many purposes, especially for cut flowers. The most usual colours are a golden-orange but there are numerous two-coloured or even multi-coloured hybrids, in shades ranging from a creamy-white, to yellow, red and lilac-pink.

202 Euphorbia (Yellow Spurge)

A family of medicinal plants containing a large number of varieties, which originates from South-eastern Europe. Some require mild and warm climates., and some an even hot-house temperature; *Euphorbia pulcherrima* for example. Many thrive in the garden. This species is perennial, and it is as beautiful in April-May with its bracteate leaves round its flowers, as it is in the autumn. In a sunny exposure the leaves take on a bright red tint. They are excellent both for rockeries and for dry and sunny flower beds. Their height is 16 ins., and the plants should be spaced 16-18 ins. apart.

203 Filipendulina (spiraea) venusta

Originally from North America, it has not long been regarded as a garden-flower. It grows 4½ ft high and flowers in July and August. It favours a dampish soil, and is often grown round lakes and ponds. It is a good plant for flower beds and for cutting.

204 Filipendulina (spiraea) hexa-petala

Prefers drier ground and a sunny exposure. It flowers from May to July and grows 20 ins. high. It is suitable for growing in beds of perennials also in rock gardens. The roots have ovoidal enlargements, which are both edible and astringent.

205 Fritillaria imperialis
(Crown Imperial)

Although this attractive flower comes originally from Persia and Turkey, it can stand up to most climates, even that of the Northern regions of Europe. The bulbs should be planted in the

158

autumn, 6 ins. deep, in sunny flower beds. They flower from late March to May, and are 2½ -4 ft high. Shortly after flowering, the leaves of the plant fade, and it is advisable to place other summer plants close to the fritillarias, so that no empty spaces remain.

206 Galanthus nivalis (*Snowdrop*)

The Latin name recalls the very special message of these little winter flowers, the Snowdrops, well-named the 'heralds of spring'. Gala is the Greek for milk and Anthos for flower. This simple milk-white flower grows wild in a great part of Europe, and in Western Asia, and quickly becomes naturalised. The bulbs should be planted in the autumn at about 1½-2 ins. deep, and should not be placed too closely together, for they increase freely in positions which suit them. They flower very early, in February-March.

207 Fritillaria meleagris
(*Fritillary or Snake's Head Lily*)

This wild plant grows in a great many places where the soil is damp. It should be planted in the autumn, preferably in a flower bed or near a lawn. A rather damp soil and halfshade should be given, and the flowers appear in April-May. The height varies according to the situation from 9-12 ins.

208 Gaillardia grandiflora
(*Blanket Flower*)

This hardy perennial is a sturdy growing plant. Nevertheless, for all its life and colour, it does not always with stand the assaults of the winter, especially if its situation is too damp. Its height is from 16-24 ins., and the diameter of its flowers from 1½-4 ins. Excellent for flower beds, and for cutting, being both decorative and lasting.

209 Galega officinalis (*Goat's Rue*)

From Southern Europe and Western

Asia. It thrives in well cultivated situations, and prefers a good depth of soil. It likes the sun. Flowering from June to August, its height is 3-5 ft. The variety called *hartlandii* is the general favourite, with its lavender-blue and white flowers. It should be protected during very hard winters if its situation is damp.

210 Gentiana acaulis (*Gentian*)

The 'stemless' Gentian appears to derive its name from a King of Illyria called Gentius who, according to Pliny, discovered the medicinal uses of the gentian plant. This type of plant is to be found very frequently in the colder regions of the Northern hemisphere; many kinds can live in the mountainous districts; and some even grow as high up as the eternal snowline. The name *Gentiana acaulis* does not cover a single variety but a whole group of similar or neighbouring types or species, such as the *G. clusii*, *G. angustifolia*, *G. alpina* or the *G. kochiana*. All these gentians favour limestone soil and sunny aspects. They flower from May to August, and all form clumps and are suitable for rockeries. Worth special mention is the *Gentiana sino-ornata*, with its abundant and beautiful flowers in the autumn which last for a long time when cut. Unlike the previous species, they prefer a soil rich in leaf mould or peat-moss.

211 Geranium endressii (*Cranesbill*)

This is originally from the Pyrenees and near by. It is a good hardy geranium for flower beds, flowering from late May to August, Its height is 18 ins. It has the advantage that while liking plenty of sun it is indifferent to the nature of its soil.

212-214 Geums (*Avens*)

These are free flowering perennials.

They have lovely colours, and like sun but grow also in the semi-shade, and most soils. Their foliage lasts all the winter.

212 Geum heldreichii

Flowering in May and June. Height 12 ins. They are excellent for rockeries.

213 Geum
'Mrs. Bradshaw'

This flowers later in June-September, and its height is double No. 212. It is one of the best for flower beds, and a good flower for cutting and lasting.

2 4 Geum
'Lady Stratheden'

This flowers from June-August. Its height is 28 ins., and the diameter of the flowers is about an inch. Suitable for cutting and for flower beds.

215 Gladiolus (Sword Lily)
large flowering hybrids

Most species originate in South Africa, although many of the excellent named hybrids have been raised in Britain. The corms should be planted early in April, at 2-3 ins. deep and 6-8 ins. apart, in any soil, though they favour a good loam which remains moist and a sunny aspect. They should be protected from the wind. The early varieties flower in June and the late in September. Their height varies greatly, from 16 ins. to 5 ft. The corms should be dug up in the autumn, dried, and put under cover for protection against the frost. They are suitable for use in several different ways, but especially for cutting. They are becoming popular in many countries. They can also be grown in the cool greenhouse. The finest of these flowers are grown from corms of the 10-12 cm. size.

216 Godetia 'Sybil Sherwood'

This is an excellent annual for flower beds which originates from California. It should be sown where it is to flower, thinning out the seedlings to 6 ins. apart. Very free flowering from June to late August. Height 9 ins. There are many varieties of godetia, both single and double.

217 Gypsophila elegans

This is an annual and originally from Asia Minor. Its height is from 12-20 ins. In rich soil, the plants become very bushy. They flower in July and are good for cutting. They should be planted where they are to flower. Thin to 6 ins. apart.

218 Gypsophila paniculata
(Chalk Plant)

This originates in Southern Europe and in Asia, and is a perennial, very valuable for the garden. It has a long and thick tap-root, which is easily injured in digging up. It is propagated by seed and by division of the roots. It favours an alkaline soil, and a sunny aspect or half-shade. Its height is from 2½-4 ft, and it flowers from June to August. It is excellent for flower beds and for cutting. There are several types with pink or double flowers. In order to preserve their characteristics, grafting or cuttings are used.

219-222 Helenium Hybridum
(Sneezeweed)

These perennials are excellent flowers for cutting and for the flower bed, and need a well drained soil as well as a sunny aspect. They put up well with drought and should be dug up every two or three years and divided, otherwise the flowers decrease in size. They are best covered in winter, and should be supported in windy aspects.

219 Helenium
'Crimson Beauty'

Flowering July to September. They have a height of 2 ft, and the diameter of their flowers is 1½ ins. They are among the first rank of perennials.

220 Helenium pumilum magnificum

Flowering July to September. One of best for cutting and blooms freely. Its height reaches 4 ft, and the diameter of its flowers is 1¾ ins.

221 Helenium
'Chipperfield Orange'

This variety flowers from August to October. Height is 5 ft. It is suitable for cutting as well as for the back row of beds of perennials.

222 Helenium
'Moerheim Beauty'

This grows 3 ft high, and flowers from July to August. This is quite the best variety for general use.

223 Helianthus bismarckianus
(Sunflower)

This variety hails from the U.S.A. It may, justifiably, be called 'Giant' for it reaches 7½-10½ feet. It should be sown in well-manured soil; and blooms from July to September. Its flowers are often over a foot wide.

224 Helianthus annuus

This is not so much grown as No. 223 and is not as large.

225 Helianthus rigidis

This gracious perennial flowers plentifully, and is good for cutting. It sometimes presents difficulties in flower beds since its short roots spread wide.

226 Helichrysum bracteatum
(Everlasting Flower)

This flower comes originally from Australia. An annual, it can be sown in the ground direct, as soon as the frosts have past. It should be thinned out to 8 or 9 ins. apart. This plant grows to a height of 3 ft. It flowers July to September. It prefers a sunny exposure. The petals have a remarkable quality of keeping both their form and colour if they are carefully cut and dried as soon as they have opened.

227 Heliopsis scabra patula

Originates from America and needs a good situation. It flowers in August and September, but needs ground not too dry. It grows about 4 ft high, and the flowers last for a long time.

228 Heliotropium peruvianum
(Heliotrope or Cherry Pie)

Originates, as its name indicates, in South America, and should be planted in groups, preferably with red and yellow flowers alongside. It can be increased by starting seeds or cuttings in the greenhouse. This plant needs sun and warmth. It flowers all the summer and has a delightful perfume. It should be grown in light and dampish ground.

229 Helleborus abchasicus
(Hellebore)

This comes from the Caucasus. It makes a wonderful effect in the half-light in rockeries, and in the front row of beds and shrubberies. It needs a moist, acid ground and the leaves last all the winter though they must be covered during severe frost. Its height is about 8 or 9 ins. It flowers in March and April.

230 Helleborus niger *(Christmas Rose*

It is generally agreed that the Christmas Rose comes from parts of Central Europe. This plant prefers the half shade and deep soil mixed with peat. It needs watering in drought, and the leaves lasts all the winter. It is prefer able to cover them during hard frosts. It flowers January-April and may even flower from late December. It needs the same general cultivation as the previous species. In certain districts Christmas Roses are grown indoors. Varieties specially recommended are the following: *praecox, altifolius, macranthus, keesen,* and *buis.*

231 Hemerocallis hybridus
(Day Lily)

The word hybrid refers to a quantity of horticultural varieties which issue from a number of the crossings between a dozen different types. These varieties are more beautiful than the absolutely pure species of plants, and often easier to grow. They accept situations which do not correspond exactly with their usual requirements. These plants favour the half-light, and dampish ground. In fact, they grow very well round sheets of water, beds of perennials, and also in isolated groups. Their height varies from 1½-4 ft, and they flower June-September. Their flower diameter is 1½-5 ins. Good varieties are the following: 'Yellow Buttercup', 'Orange Dawn', 'George Yeld', with its big orange buttercups, 'Margaret Perry', yellow and orange, and 'Sir Michael Foster', lemon-yellow.

232 Hesperis matronalis
(Sweet Rocket)

This originates in South America, and is full of perfume. It is easy to cultivate, will grow everywhere and does particularly well in beds of perennials. It flowers May-June. Height 2¾ ft.

233 Hepatica *(Hungarian Anemone)*

This originates, as its name indicates, from Hungary. It is larger than the *Hepatica triloba;* both prefer a damp and half-shaded position. Its height is 6 ins., and it flowers in March-April.

234 Hepatica triloba *double rose*

This is grown much the same as the preceding variety but it will also grow well in full sun. It is larger than *Hepatica triloba* itself and gives a most generous effect in the rockery and in odd corners. Its height is 4 ins., and it flowers in March and April.

235 Heuchera brizoides
(Alum Root or Coral Bells)

This species comprises about 35 kinds from South America and Mexico, and is excellent for rockeries, borders, and for cut flowers. It likes ground which is somewhat damp. Height 12 ins. It flowers June-July.

236 Hosta ventricosa *(Plantain Lily)*

This may be grown in many places, particularly by ponds and lakes, and near banks of rhododendrons. It enjoys full sun or half-light and rich soil which is rather damp. It is mostly grown for its foliage. The fine flowers appear in August-September at a height of 2 ft; sometimes the fully developed leaves reach 2¼ ft.

237 Hosta lancifolia

This plant is used much the same as the previous one. Its height is from 1½-1¾ ft, and it flowers during August-September, but needs planting closer than does the *Hosta ventricosa.* The variety albo-marginata, striped with white, is finer than the rest.

238-243 Hyacinths

Many hyacinth bulbs are now planted in gardens and they are no longer used solely as greenhouse bulbs, for they grow outdoors in soil which is rich and nourishing. They should be planted 4-5 ins. deep in September-October. To obtain the best effect, they should not be more than 6 ins. apart. They can be sheltered from frosts by a cover of dead leaves, but in that case may need protection against vermin. They flower in April-May and the leaves should not be removed until they have faded, and that is the time when the bulbs should be dug and stored until autumn. They can be used alone or with any other flowers. The best spots for these blooms are flower beds or as edging for perennial borders.

238 Hyacinth
'*Lady Derby*'

This is a good kind for gardens, and for early flowering. Most reliable.

239 Hyacinth
'*La Victoire*'

This is good for a early display, indeed it is one of the best varieties of 'red tones'.

240 Hyacinth
'*Queen of the Pinks*'

This is a beautiful variety which is strong growing and lasts well. The bulbs themselves seem also to remain strong and healthy for years.

241 Hyacinth
'*City of Haarlem*'

The yellow types are, generally speaking, the most fragile. This one is the best of its colour.

242 Hyacinth
'*Grand Maitre*'

This is fairly early and excellent of its kind. Its colour stands valiantly against the sun's rays.

243 Hyacinth
'*L'Innocence*'

This is one of the oldest of its race. It flowers early and has an agreeable perfume.

244 Iberis *(Candytuft)*
'*Snowflake*'

This originates in the South of Europe and is a perennial. Like a small shrub, it produces much bushy growth. It makes a great effect in rockeries with alyssum and phlox, and the leaves remain green all the winter, though they need covering if in a very exposed spot. Enough space should be left to each plant to develop, for it does so very considerably. Its height is from 8-12 ins.

245 Iberis umbellata purpurea

This originates in Southern Europe and is an annual. At the beginning of the spring it should be sown where it is to flower, in a warm and sunny place. It flowers from May to August. Height 12 ins. Excellent for edges and borders.

246 Impatiens balsamina
(Balsam or Touch-me-not)

In order to assure full development and a lasting effect, it is necessary to sow under a frame at the end of March. It may then be put into its proper place in June and stopped at 12 ins. It flowers from June-October, but is easily spoiled by the frosts. The flower stems reach from 12-20 ins. in height. It is to be found in all colours, single, semi-double or fully double.

247 Incarvillea delavayi

This flower, as its name somewhat suggests, originates in China. Its height reaches 27 ins. and the bunches are often composed of 10 to 12 flowers each 2¼ ins. long. It flowers in June-July.

248 Ipomaea purpurea
(Morning Glory)

This originates in America, and is an annual creeper; it may be sown where it is to flower though it is better if sown under glass. It is much used for covering verandahs and fences. The height of this fine creeper may reach 12 ft during the summer. It flowers from June until the frosts, with a great display of colour, and it benefits from the full sun.

249 Iris pumila

This originates in Southern Europe. The dwarf irises of horticulturists are the result of the crossings of various types. They are used especially in rockeries, and indeed the full effect is best if they are grouped together in patches. The rhizomes should be placed horizontally without being completely covered with soil, selecting a sunny spot. It has no other special needs of soil and it flowers April-June at a height of some 4-8 ins.

250 Iris pseudacorus

This generous flower grows wild almost all over Europe, Northern Africa and Western Asia. In its natural state it lives in marshy lands and by the lakeside, though it can be grown in almost any spot with a sunny aspect. It is most useful in conjunction with other plants. It must be planted relatively deep and flowers in June-July, growing 3 ft high.

251 Iris reticulata

This originates in the Caucasus and by its very narrow flowers, it differs quite distinctly from all the other irises mentioned here. It needs planting in light and porous, peaty soil in the full sun. One single plant can become the origin of an important group. Plant 4 ins. deep. The flowering time is January to April. The leaves reach 15 ins. in length. Very suitable for rockeries.

252 Iris siberica

Originating whence its name suggests,

it is used above all others around wet marshy spots, where it has room to spread, and is also suitable for flower beds. It flowers in June, at a height of from 20-36 ins.

253-261 Iris germanica

The result of divers crossings of different horticulturists and indeed few plants possess such diverse forms with such rich and varied colours. In France, Belgium and England, specialists in horticulture offer several hundreds of different kinds. There are, indeed, many books devoted to the subject of the iris. It is a fact that a collection of the best irises can be more costly than a collection of orchids, though their culture is easy, and they have few needs as regards soil. They like the sun, but grow also in the shade. It is better not to cover the rhizomes completely. They flower from May to July, according to the variety.

253 Iris germanica
'Madame Chereau'

This flower grows to a height of about 32 ins. and is free flowering. It is excellent for flower beds, but is not among the earliest flowering.

254 Iris germanica
'Madame Gaudichau'

This flowers at a height of 3 feet, and has very large blooms, but is rather late.

255 Iris germanica
'Clematis'

Height 28 ins. Free flowering and mid-season.

256 Iris germanica
'Flamboyant'

Height 32 ins. It flowers in June, making a good display in flower beds.

257 Iris germanica, odoratissima

The height of this plant is 3 ft, and it has flowers over 4 ins. wide. This is one of the very best among the mauves.

258 Iris germanica
'La Beaute'

This flower is 28 ins. high and of a very pure colour. It is relatively late blooming

259 Iris germanica
'Mrs. Neubrunner'

This flower is 28 ins. high and a mid-season sort. It shows up best when mixed with red and blue varieties.

260 Iris germanica
'Rota'

The height of this plant is 20 ins., and it is relatively late. It is very free flowering and certainly one of the best among the reds.

261 Iris germanica
'Rheine Traube'

The height of this plant is 32 ins., and its flower is 4 ins. wide. It is a late variety.

262 Kniphofia 'The Rocket'
(Red Hot Poker)

This originates in South Africa, where there are numerous types of kniphofia. The horticultural varieties are the result of a certain number of 'crossings' between these and they need to be grown in moist soil and given protection in winter. The kniphofias are suitable for flower beds, but need sun and congenial conditions. They look well in groups and among the hybrids 'The Rocket' is considered one of the very best. Its height is 3 ft, and the length of the flower head is from 8-12 ins. It flowers in August-September.

263 Kniphofia 'Royal Standard'

This hybrid is quite the most robust among these types and one of the few which has any value as a flower for cutting. It is also the easiest to grow. Its height is from 3-4 ft. It flowers in August and September and its growth and uses are the same as those of the previous type.

264 Kochia trichophylla

In order to obtain fine specimens, it is necessary to sow seed under glass, and then put the plants into a rich, warm position in June. For borders, they are better spaced 10 ins. apart, in other places allow 15 ins. between the plants. In autumn this plant assumes a striking red colour. It is a native of Southern Europe, and in Northern latitudes it does not usually ripen its seed pods in the open.

265 Lathyrus odoratus
(Sweet Pea)

This flower grows wild in Southern Italy and in Sicily, and produces two or three fair-sized flowers on short stalks. Our modern kinds produce stems having 4 to 6 large flowers on a length of from 8-12 ins. The whole art of growing sweet peas consists in putting them into good soil of at least 2 ft in depth. If the soil happens to be un-favourable, then it is better to dig a trench and to fill it with good compost and manure. Sowing can be done where the plants are to flower, or with still better results in pots. The flowering period is June to September. Sweet peas make up very attractive bouquets.

266 Lathyrus latifolius
(Everlasting Pea)

This flower is from Southern Europe, but it is perfectly naturalised over a great part of this country. It is, how-ever, scentless. With sufficient supports, the plant reaches a height of 6 ft during the summer. The flowering time is June to September. In Northern regions it is wise to cover it over, during the winter.

267 Lathyrus vernus

This begins to flower in April, when the plants are 2-3 ins. high, and the flowering goes on into May. The plants grow 16 ins. high. This subject is suitable for flower beds, but like the previous types needs a sunny aspect.

268 Lavatera trimestris *(Mallow)*

This flower originates in the Mediterranean regions, and should be sown where it is to flower and stopped at 12 ins. It flowers from July to September and is suitable for flower beds. It prefers, above all, a rather dry and stony soil and reaches a height of 3 ft.

269 Leontopodium alpinum
(Edelweiss)

This plant is a native of the Alps and is very easy to grow. It prefers stony soil and a sunny position without any shade, and is very effective in rockeries. It reaches to a height of 8 ins., and flowers from June to September.

270 Leucojum vernum *(Snowflake)*

This flower grows wild in many countries. The bulbs should be planted in August and September, 4 ins. deep, in groups of four, so as to constitute small clumps. It then increases in quantity and has the same uses as the snowdrop. It makes an excellent effect under bushes, and flowers from February to April. It grows 6 ins. high.

271 Liatris spicata
(Blazing Star or Button Snakeroot)

This flower originates in North America and makes a very bright effect in flower beds. It likes ordinary garden soil and prefers semi-shade, though it grows quite well in the sun. It flowers from July to September. Height 2½ ft, with the length of the flower spikes 14 ins.

272-277 Lilium *(Lily)*

The growing of most lilies is quite simple, though some principles must be followed in order to obtain good results. It would seem that for most varieties the quantity of alkali or acid in the soil has no great importance. However, if the bulbs are to be placed in chalky soil or heavy ground, it is wise to add some turfy loam and sandy soil. The bulbs should be planted at about three times their own depth. During their period of growth lilies require plenty of moisture. The soil may be shaded by small, low growing plants. Many lilies like to grow under trees which afford some slight shelter.

272 Lilium candidum
(Madonna Lily)

Originates in Eastern Mediterranean Regions. It should be planted less deeply than the other types, an inch of soil above the bulbs being sufficient. It flowers in July, and generally produces about twenty flowers of nearly 2 ins. in width, on stems of 4-5 ft high. It is highly scented, but should not be transplanted unless really necessary.

273 Lilium martagon

This lily grows wild in the French mountains, and looks well when placed with other alpine plants or in parts of a garden that are allowed to run a little wild. There are from 20-30 flowers on each stem, which are from 3-4 ft high.

274 Lilium regale *(Regal Lily)*

This was discovered for the first time in 1888 in China in the Yunnan and then again in 1903 in the Setchuen. It is from bulbs imported this second time that all the Royal lilies of today are derived. This is certainly the lily which is grown the most widely at present. It blooms towards the end of July and the flowers, which are delicately scented, are 3 ins. wide, 12-20 appearing on each stem.

275 Lilium tigrinum *(Tiger Lily)*

This flower has its origin in Eastern Asia. It has no special requirements. It flowers in July-August, growing 5 ft high, with 12 or more flowers on each stem.

276 Lilium umbellatum
'*Darkest of all*'

This variety has been grown for a long time past, in several shades of colour. It flowers in June and July at a height of 2 ft, and has no special needs.

277 Lilium umbellatum
'*Golden Fleece*'

This lily is as easy to grow as the previous one. Its height is 2 ft, and it flowers in July, having large florets up to 2 ins. wide.

278 Linaria pallida *(Toadflax)*

This flax plant is similar to the toad flax commonly known as the 'Ruin of Rome', but its flowers are twice as large. It is one of the best plants for covering walls, for its seeds slip between the very stones and soon increase in size and strength. It flowers chiefly in May and June.

279 Linum perenne *(Flax)*

This flower is suitable for inclusion in a flower bed of perennials. Sun is required for best results. It flourishes better in stony soil, and grows 18-28 ins. high. The flowers appear in June-August. It is of little use for cutting, since the petals fall quickly.

280 Linum grandiflorum

This plant has its origin in Algeria, and is an annual. It should be sown in April and May where it is to flower. It grows 15-20 ins. high and flowers from June to August. Pretty in the garden, it is of little use for cutting.

281 Lobelia erinus

This flower has its origin in Southern Africa and should be sown under glass at the beginning of March. It can be planted in its flowering quarters in its summer home during May. It will flower from June until the frosts come. Good soil and a sunny aspect are necessary. This flower is very suitable for edging beds and borders.

282 Lobelia hybrida pendula
(trailing)

The hybrid is grown like the previous one and suits pots and flower-boxes. It flowers all the summer, and the hanging growths reach a length of 12 ins.

283 Lupinus polyphyllus *(Lupin)*
mixed

This plant has its origin in North America, but this variety is grown less and less often, and since 1938 the 'Russell Hybrids' have replaced it. This is because of the variety of the colours, and of the size and quality of their flower spikes. As perennials they constitute one of the most useful plants of our gardens. They grow to a height of 3 ft, with the floral stem 16 ins. high. Flowering from June to August, the plants should be lightly protected in exposed places during the winter, though they have no special requirements as to soil. They do prefer a sunny aspect.

284 Lychnis chalcedonica
(Jerusalem Cross or Scarlet Lychnis)

This plant originates from Eastern

Europe and from Asia. It can well be grown with the delphinium. It prefers a well-manured soil and the maximum of sun, and should not be transplanted too often. Flowering from June to July, it grows 3 ft high.

285 Lychnis coronaria *(Rose Campion)*

This flower comes from Southern Europe and is perennial, although it is treated as biennial, and the second crop of flowers is finer than the first. It has no special needs as to soil, but prefers a sunny aspect if possible. It is very suitable for flower beds of perennials, and is continuous in flowering. It has roughish, grey leaves and grows to a height of 28 ins. Its flowering is from the beginning of June until the end of the summer.

286 Lysimachia nummularia *(Creeping Jenny)*

This popular plant grows wild in many parts of France and Northern Europe, as well as Central Europe and the Caucasus. It prefers, above all, rather dampish and semi-shaded ground. Its stems creep along the ground to form a more or less dense carpet on the soil. It will also serve well for covering a wall, in flower boxes or in frames, and is absolutely at home in rockeries. Flowers from June to the end of August.

287 Lysimachia punctata *(Yellow Loosestrife)*

This plant coming from Central and Eastern Europe, makes a charming appearance in flower beds among other perennials. It has a preference for dampish and semi-shaded ground. It looks well placed with *astilbe*, *lythrum* and *Salvia nemorosa*. Its flowering period is July and August.

288 Lythrum salicaria 'Rose Queen' *(Purple Loosestrife)*

This plant is good for supplying flowers for cutting. It should be planted relatively close, at 12-15 ins. apart in good garden soil, in the sun or semi-shade. It flowers from June to September.

289 Macleaya (Bocconia) cordata *(Plume Poppy)*

This plant comes originally from Western Asia. Its very decorative foliage will last all the summer. It may be placed either at the back of beds of perennials or in beds on its own, in the middle of a lawn, or mixed among other plants. It is a very healthy plant and accepts all kinds of soils and aspects. It increases fairly rapidly in size, through its underground parts. It reaches a height of 7½ ft, and flowers in July-August.

290 Malope trifida

Originally from North Africa, this flower is an annual. It is very like the great mallow (*Lavatera trimestris*), but is much less subject to ailments than the latter. It should be sown where it is to flower and thinned to 15 ins. apart. It accepts all kinds of ground, but likes plenty of sun. It flowers in July and August, very abundantly. It is 3 ft high. This flower exists in red and yellow as well as in white.

291 Matricaria eximia

This is certainly one of the most floriferous and one of the easiest summer plants to grow. It should be sown under glass first and then replanted in the open 8 ins. apart. The flowering period is between June to October, and it may be transplanted in the midst of flowering, if it is plentifully watered.

292 Matthiola incana annua *(Ten Week Stock)*

Originally from Southern Europe, this plant owes its popularity to its fragrant perfume. Only the single flowers produce seed. In spite of a severe selection, it has not been possible to obtain a proportion of more than 60 % of the total in the double flowers. Given a sunny aspect, it is possible to sow where the plants are to flower, though it is still better to sow under glass. If the young plants are kept in too much damp they are liable to be attacked by damping off disease. They need good soil, and a sunny aspect, and are suitable for flower beds and for cutting. The best known varieties are the 'Nice', 'Victoria' and 'Excelsior', which all exist in various colours, at a height of 10-28 ins., and they flower between May and September.

293 Mimulus cupreus
(Musk or Monkey Flower)

This flower comes from Chile, is perennial, very beautiful and most floriferous. Placed around pools and ponds, or in rockeries, it flowers well at a height of 8 ins., May-October.

294 Mimulus tigrinus hybridus

This flower is an annual and should be sown under glass; it can then be planted in its outdoor home when all risk of frost is reasonably past. It needs rich soil, retentive of moisture, and is suitable for groups, flower beds or in rockeries. Flowering is from July to August and plants grow to 12 ins.

295 Meconopsis betonicifolia
(Himalayan Poppy or Blue Poppy)

This flower comes originally from East Asia. The type known as Baileyi is perennial, so long as the plants are not allowed to flower the first year. It should be planted in well drained, acid soil, preferably semi-shaded. It is better covered in winter, and flowers in June-July. The width of the flowers is 4 ins.

and the height of the plant 3 ft.

296 Menyanthes trifoliata
(Bog Bean)

This is a plant for marshy places, and is spread over a wide part of the Northern Hemisphere. It is useful for planting around pools and ponds. The decorative flowers are seen from April to July, and grow to a height of 12 ins.

297 Montbretia crocosmiiflora

This montbretia is the result of the crossing of two types— Crocosmia aurea and Tritonia pottsii. The plants may be left in the earth in the winter, but should be covered during the frosts in very cold regions. Suitable for borders and for flower beds, they may be planted with 'Viola Cornuta', which forms both an undergrowth and a protection for the winter. They attain a height of 28 ins., and flower from July until the frosts. This is a plant which is good for cutting.

298 Monarda didyma 'Cambridge Scarlet' (Bergamot or Bee Balm)

This comes originally from North America, and is excellent for flower beds, as it has a long period of flowering. It must be planted in dampish soil, in the sun or semi-shade. The leaves, just like the flowers, have a strong scent. The flowers produce 'monardine', colouring matter. They flower during June and July, and grow 2½-3 ft high.

299 Myosotis sylvatica
(Forget-me-not)

This plant grows wild in the woods and fields of hilly regions. The stronger horticultural forms have larger and more flowers. They are usually grown as biennials, and they can be moved quite easily, as with pansies. They should be sown in June, and planted out in July in the nursery, and they can then be put into their final place the next spring. If conditions suit them, they multiply freely. They flower May to July, and reach a height of 8-12 ins.

300 Myosotis palustris

This flower grows wild in marshy regions. It should be grown as the former variety, but is better bedded around ponds. It will begin to flower when the *Myosotis sylvatica* are on the decline, and continue until autumn.

301 Muscari botryoides
(Grape Hyacinth)

There are fifty-odd types of grape hyacinth in the Mediterranean regions, and *Muscari botryoides* is one of the most beautiful. The bulbs should be planted 4 ins. deep in September or October, and they have no special needs. The flowering time is March to May, and the height 4-6 ins.

302-309 Narcissus

Two different interpretations are suggested for this name Narcissus. According to the first, the flower is called after the young Greek, Narcissus, who in the legend, was changed into the flower; but the other explanation merely suggests that the name comes from the Greek word 'narke', which means 'torpor'. There are about 40 types known scattered throughout Europe and in the Mediterranean Regions. Innumerable varieties and hybrids, have been, and are still being created. The bulbs should be planted early in August and September up to 5 ins. deep. Narcissi like their soil to be rich, light and fresh, with a sunny exposure in general, or, in certain cases, slightly shaded. The leaves should be preserved until they have faded. They make a pretty impression in clumps under bushes, in beds of perennials, or right in the front of walls or hedges.

Their average height is 12-15 ins., and they flower generally, during April-May, while a few varieties show colour in February and March.

302 Narcissus tazzetta

This variety has white petals and gives a charming effect when mixed with other flowers of a bright colour.

303 Narcissus poetaz
'Scarlet Gem'

This is rather early, and is pleasantly scented.

304 Narcissus poetaz
'Laurens Koster'

Free flowering, and rather early. Has a perfect carriage.

305 Narcissus poeticus
'Actaea'

This variety is highly scented, but flowers rather late. It has the advantage that it can be placed in meadowland, since cattle do not touch it.

306 Narcissus
'Scarlet Elegance'

This narcissus, sometimes called 'The Incomparable', is midway, as it were, between the *Narcissus-pseudo-Narcissus* and *Narcissus poeticus*. It is semi-late in flowering, but has a peculiar perfume of its own.

307 Narcissus
'Golden Harvest'

One of the best single yellow narcissi. It is late but strong growing.

308 Narcissus
'Spring Glory'

This flower is a remarkable improvement on the old bicolor 'Victoria'. It is early and very vigorous as well as free flowering.

309 Nɘrcissus
'*Van Sion*'

This is an old and very well-known variety: it is semi-early.

310 Nemesia strumosa
mixed

Originally from South Africa, this plant should be sown under glass in the early spring, and planted outdoors in April or May. The seedlings should be spaced 6 ins. apart. The flowering period is June to September, and the plants grow 10-12 ins. high. This type is suitable for flower-beds, borders and balconies.

311 Nemophila insignis
(*Baby Blue Eyes*)

Originally from California, this plant is an annual. It makes fine bushy plants. Seed can be sown in the open in a sunny aspect thinning the seedlings to 6 ins. apart. The flowering time is June to August. Suitable for borders and flower beds.

312 Nepeta mussini (*Catmint*)

Originally from the Caucasus, this is an excellent flower for a border. It prefers well drained soil and a sunny exposure. It should be planted in the spring, and before the stalks of the previous year are cut the new shoots should be allowed to commence growing. Flowering end of May-July, 15 ins. high. Strongly scented, this is a medical plant.

313 Nicotiana sanderae (*Tobacco*)

Originally the nicotine or tobacco plant comes from Brazil. The flowers are scentless, but they open even during the sunny hours of the day. This plant is annual and needs sowing early in the spring under glass. It can then be planted out at the end of May, and spaced 15 ins. apart. It prefers a warm, light soil and a sunny exposure.

314 Nigella damascena
(*Love-in-a-mist*)

Picturesquely named, the plant grows wild in Mediterranean regions as well as in Northern Africa, and right into Asia Minor. It should be sown where it is to flower and thinned to 4 ins. apart. It will flower in June and July, and attains a height of 20 ins. It should be noted that even after the flowering the foliage still remains decorative.

315-318 Nymphaea (*Water Lily*)

It seemed to us better to keep the word Nuphar or Yellow Pond Lily for the yellow flowers, and to name the second type Nymphaeas or White Water Lily. It is the second type we are dealing with in Nos. 315-318. The White Water Lily grows wild in ponds and very slow moving streams. Water lilies with pink and red flowers do exist, and the hybrids especially are grown. They should be grown in still and sunny water, planted first in closely woven baskets. The kind of soil is of little importance, provided only that it holds the compost firmly. We shall show later, for each type, the most favourable depth of water. If the Nymphaeas are grown in cemented basins, which have to be emptied during the winter, the plants should be kept in receptacles with very little water, and in cool cellars. The roots, however, should not be left in dry basins and above all should not be covered with dead leaves, for then mice would attack them. The flowers only open out in the sunlight.

315 Nymphaea '*James Brydon*'

This hybrid type of water lily needs growing in 28-40 ins. of water. It is strong and very floriferous.

316 Nymphaea alba

This species is specially intended for

ornamental ponds and lakes, and can be planted in water 3 ft or more in depth. Established plants cover a large surface.

317 Nymphaea marliacea
'*Chromatella*'

This water lily should be under water from 2½—4½ ft deep. It spreads relatively slowly, but it has pretty brown-red leaves.

318 Nymphaea '*Escarboucle*'

This should be grown in water 2-3 ft deep. It grows fairly fast. It has a marvellous red flower with golden-yellow stamens in the centre.

319 Oenothera glauca
'*Fraseri*'

This has greenish-yellow flowers and comes from North America. A perennial, it likes all kinds of soil where there is a sunny aspect. Its height is 20 ins., and its blooms are nearly 2 ins. wide. It flowers in July-August in abundance, and presents a charming appearance in the front row of perennials.

320 Oenothera missouriensis

This plant, which also comes from North America, likes dry ground and full sun as far as possible. Transplanting rather old plants should be avoided, since they only possess, one single taproot which easily breaks. It flowers a long time, right up until the frosts, and the width of the flowers is over 3 ins. This is a plant for rockeries, walls, and the front row of perennial flower beds.

321 Omphalodes verna
(*Navelwort*)

This plant comes originally from Central Europe, but has now become naturalised in several countries. It is perennial, and prefers a good, peaty soil and semi-shade. Reaching a height

of from 4-6 ins., it flowers over a long period from March to May. It is best placed on the north aspect of rockeries or shrubberies.

322 Ornithogalum nutans
(*Star of Bethlehem*)

This flower grows wild in Europe and in Asia Minor. It is especially a plant which is ideal for putting in parts of gardens which are to be left unattended. It does not always flower very abundantly. It prefers the semi-shade and damp, and attains 12 ins. in height, the width of each flower being an inch. The heads often consist of 12 flowers which appear in April and May.

323-331 Paeonia (*Peony*)

The peony is best planted in the autumn in well enriched soil, previously manured, and in spots which are sunny and open. The young crowns should not be covered with more than 2 ins. of soil, and should be dug up only when the clumps need dividing, which is usually from 6-10 years. Bone meal or other organic fertiliser is better for these varieties than farmyard manure. If the flower stems are too heavy, they need supporting as soon as their buds break. The foliage must not be taken away before it has faded. Peonies must be included among the most magnificent of garden flowers, but they do not fit in with other flowers. It is better then, to plant them by themselves in clumps among shrubs, or in completely isolated groups. Peonies of the group 'albiflora', give a strong and pleasant perfume. The flowering period is June and July, and they are excellent flowers for cutting. The type which gave birth to this variety came originally from China. Some garden hybrid peonies give an odour which is not agreeable. These flower from April-June.

323 Paeonia albiflora
'MacMahon'

This type is of English origin. It attains a height of 3 ft, with flowers nearly 3 ins. wide. It is semi-early, and very abundant in flowers.

324 Paeonia
'Queen Wilhelmina'

This type has silky petals, and is rather early. It attains a height of 30 ins., and its flowers are 5 ins. wide.

325 Paeonia
'Couronne d'Or'

This flower has a height of 3 ft, and is rather late. It is one of the very best among the yellow varieties, and, it should be noted, that there are but few of these.

326 Paeonia officinalis
double rose

This variety attains a height of 24 ins., and is easy to grow. It is early, and has few requirements. Its very large flowers are over 7 ins. in diameter.

327 Paeonia officinalis
double red

This is one of our oldest garden plants, and is early flowering. It grows 2 ft high.

328 Paeonia albiflora
'Kashna-no-Mai'

This comes from Japan, and is a mid-season variety. The height is 3 ft, and the flowers, which are single or semi-double, are in the most delicate shades.

329 Paeonia albiflora
'Kasugano'

The Kasugano peony is also of Japanese origin. It is very elegant and outstanding. It reaches a height of 3 ft, and is very free flowering.

330 Paeonia albiflora
'Whitleyi Major'

This flower resembles a giant camellia, and has the most decorative foliage. It grows 3 ft high, and it is free flowering too, but rather late.

331 Paeonia albiflora
'Avalanche'

This plant is of French origin and is a very beautiful variety. It attains a height of 3 ft, and though it is semi-late it usually flowers the first season after moving, which many perennials never do.

332 Papaver nudicaule
(Iceland Poppy)

This plant comes from the Arctic regions of the Northern Hemisphere. Though it is a perennial, it often dies after the second year. It is easily resown however, but prefers dry and stony soil, with a sunny aspect. Its height is 16 ins., and it blooms from May right until the autumn. It exists in all colours and is suitable for flower beds and rockeries.

333 Papaver orientale
(Oriental Poppy)

Originally from the Caucasus, this flower is also a perennial. It grows better if transplanted in the autumn in good, warm and well drained ground, and right in the sun. It is suitable for flower beds of perennials and should be planted, for preference, with types of perennials, which are late flowering, for the leaves of the poppies fade after the flowering, and leave empty spaces. The height of this plant is 3 ft, and the flowers are often 6 or 7 ins. wide. Among the good varieties should be mentioned the following: 'The Goliath' scarlet; 'King George', with fringed red petals, and 'Perry's White'. The flowering time is June.

334 Papaver somniferum
(Opium Poppy)

The double flowered opium poppy comes originally from the Orient, and is an annual. It must be sown where it is to flower, and spaced 8 ins. apart. It reaches a height of 2½ ft, and flowers from July-September.

335 Papaver somniferum
'Dannebrog'

This poppy is very effective when placed in groups. It attains a height of 2 ft.

336-345 Pelargonium

The name 'Pelargonium' comes from the Greek Pelargos (Stork) and recalls the shape of the beak of the storks. Over 250 types of this plant are known, the majority originally from South Africa, and there are now many different varieties and hybrids. Certain varieties are excellent for greenhouses, for balconies, and for summer bedding. The increasing is done by taking cuttings. These are taken in August, and give specimens of a good size, so formed that they can be put, with advantage, in their place in the spring. Cuttings taken in February-March also give a good display. During the winter the pots containing the plants should be kept in a light room where it is frost proof and as dry as possible without, however, allowing the leaves to fade. Then they should be planted in bigger pots in the spring. They must not be in flower when they are planted out. The site should be both sunny and sheltered. They do well in ordinary soil. In boxes and on balconies they need liquid fertiliser until July. They will generally flower from the time of their planting until the first frosts.

336 Pelargonium peltatum
'Cattleya' (Ivy-leaved Geranium)

This plant hangs or trails. It is an Ivy-leaved Pelargonium and has thick, lobed leaves. The colour of the flowers goes well with violet hybrid petunias.

337 Pelargonium peltatum
'Madame Crousse'

This French variety is widely grown. It is excellent as a creeper, having long, drooping shoots.

338 Pelargonium peltatum
'Balkan King'

This is another excellent variety and free flowering. It is suitable for many purposes.

339 Pelargonium peltatum, rubra robusta

Of a very strong bushy habit; the stems are relatively short.

340 Pelargonium zonale
'Meteor' (Zonal Geranium)

The word zonale recalls that there is a dark zone present on the foliage. 'Meteor' is one of the oldest varieties, and one of the most suitable for large clumps. It is vigorous in growth, and free flowering. It frequently attains a height as much as 3 ft during the summer.

341 Pelargonium zonale
'West Brighton Gem'

This plant is relatively low growing. It is, however, free flowering, and stands up to bad weather.

342 Pelargonium zonale
'Purple King'

An old German type. It should be planted in front of light backgrounds. Its height is from 24-28 ins.

343 Pelargonium zonale
'Leif'

This is similar to the old variety 'Lerchenmuller' but a lighter shade: it always seems to be full of flower, and grows from 16-20 ins. high.

344 Pelargonium zonale
'Poitevine Beauty'

Another free flowering variety, growing from 20-28 ins. high. It should be placed preferably against dark backgrounds.

345 Pelargonium zonale
'Madame Salleron'

This variety is generally grown more for its foliage than for its flowers, which are not very showy. But it can make a good display in borders, and attains a height of 12-16 ins.

346 Penstemon gentianoides hybrida *(Beard Tongue)*

This plant comes originally from Mexico, and though it is really a perennial, it is treated as an annual. It can be increased either in the greenhouse, by seed, or by cuttings, and can be put into the garden bed as soon as the risk of frost is over. It prefers light, warm soil, and a sunny aspect. Allow 10-12 ins. between the plants. Height 2-2½ ft. Flowering from June to September, it is suitable for flower beds or borders of perennials.

347-350 Petunia

Most varieties now grown originate from the South-American types, P. *nyctaginiflora* and P. *violacea*, the latter being perennial and semi-bushy. Although perennial, they are best treated as annuals in our climate. Sow under glass and put into flowering places when all risk of frost is past. The hybrids should have a warm and sunny aspect, but have no special requirements as to soil, though they prefer a light but fairly rich position. The spacing should be 8 or 9 ins. apart. They are suitable for clumps or for

flower beds. They also grow well in pots, and in flower boxes of all sizes.

347 Petunia
'Rose of Heaven'

This is a charming type, flowering from June to September. The height is from 8-10 ins. The colours are bright and striking.

348 Petunia
'Lavender Blue'

This variety is excellent for banks of mixed flowers. It is a sturdy plant, and free flowering.

349 Petunia violacea

An excellent variety, it has long stems which either creep or hang. It is indeed the type which is the most used for balconies, and has a pleasant perfume. The width of its flowers is over 2 ins.

350 Petunia
'Canadian Wonder'

This is a new variety with huge, elegant flowers of the most striking colours, but it is more sensitive to bad weather than the previous types. It should be put in places where it can be easily seen. Its height is 12 ins.

351 Phlox drummondii
mixed

This plant came originally from Texas, and has an abundance of flowers from May till October. Its height is from 12-24 ins. It should be sown either under glass or in the open, but in a warm and sheltered spot. Space the plants 6-10 ins. apart. It is a flower for beds, but does not last well when cut.

352-361 Phlox paniculata

This plant comes originally from North America. Though it was first brought into Europe in 1732, it was only really brought into cultivation a century later, but since then its popularity has greatly increased and a large number of hybrids and varieties have been created. In late years efforts have been made to create varieties resistant to disease and eelworm attack. In order to obtain useful results. cuttings must be inserted as soon as they are made. Phlox prefer the soil to be fairly rich, and they like to be in full sun or half-shade. When transplanted, they should be placed a little deeper than they were before, and indeed are better divided every three years in order to prevent the flowers becoming smaller, and the stems bare. These autumn flowering phlox are to be counted as among the most appreciated of garden flowers at that time of year. They may be used for flower beds, or for placing in clumps towards the front of shrubberies. A bed consisting of several plants of a number of varieties will produce a striking effect. They need spacing from 10-15 ins. apart, and will flower from July-September. They are quite hardy.

352 Phlox paniculata
'Frau Alfred von Mauthner'

This plant stands up well to rough weather. It attains a height of 28-32 ins. It has enormous panicles of flowers, each floret being more than 1½ ins. in diameter. It is rather late in flowering.

353 Phlox paniculata
'Amethyst'

This has dark foliage, and reaches a height of 3½ ft. This is also late flowering.

354 Phlox paniculata
'Jules Sandeau'

This variety is especially suitable for planting in groups. Its stem is sturdy, and it grows to a height of 20 ins. It is early and long flowering, with dense panicles, each floret being nearly 2 ins. wide.

355 Phlox paniculata
'Riverton Jewel'

This variety stands up well to drought, and is midseason in flowering. It grows to a height of 3 ft, and likes a cool situation.

356 Phlox paniculata
'Evelyn'

The height of this plant is 44 ins., but the panicles are relatively small; the width of the flowers is 2½ ins.

357 Phlox paniculata
'Hindenburg'

This plant is easy to grow and has a nice fresh appearance. It grows 3½ ft high, and is late flowering.

358 Phlox paniculata
'Fritiof'

This phlox is strong and grows 3 ft high, and blooms late. Its foliage being light green it makes a fine effect against a dark background.

359 Phlox paniculata
'Mia Ruys'

This is one of the finest of the white varieties. In general it is tall growing, and its flowers are nearly 2 ins. wide. Height 32 ins. Late flowering.

360 Phlox paniculata
'Wilhelm Kesselring'

This plant has a fresh, cool appearance, and is free flowering. Its colour is rather rare in a phlox. The width of the flower is nearly 2 ins.

361 Phlox paniculata
'Queen's Cluster'

This is a very old variety and easy to grow; it is strong, and has large panicles, although not so free flowering as some others. It grows 4 ft high.

362-365 Phlox subulata

These alpine phlox from North America are indispensable in the rockery, and are trailing and free flowering. They make a real flower carpet during April and May. Their flowers stems are from 6-8 ins. long, and they like all soils. They prefer open sunny beds, and should be planted in the autumn or very early in spring, at 8 ins. apart. Should bare spaces occur, then a little fresh soil should be introduced and news plants put in. As well as rockeries, these plants can also be grown in the front rows of beds of perennials, round ponds and miniature lakes, and especially in the front of shrubberies.

362 Phlox subulata nivalis

This is a close growing, free flowering variety.

363 Phlox subulata atropurpurea

One of the most popular and most frequently grown varieties.

364 Phlox subulata
'G. F. Wilson'

This plant is a hybrid with large flowers of rare beauty.

365 Phlox subulata 'Lilacina'

This has the most beautiful foliage, close and dense.

366 Physostegia virginiana
(Obedient Flower)

Originally from North America, these are perennials. The height reaches 4 ft or more, and the flowers, shaped like long ears of corn, have the curious characteristic that if they are moved, they are unable to take up their natural stance again, whence their popular name of 'Obedient Flower'. This plant prefers a rather damp soil, and sunny or semi-shaded aspect. The flowering period is from July to September, and the plants are suitable for flower beds. The variety 'Vivid', which is the most popular of all, grows 16-20 ins. high.

367 Phytolacca americana
(Virginian Poke)

Originally from North America but now widely grown in Britain. This is another good perennial. It will grow in any soil, though it prefers, above all others, a rather cool situation. It should have a sunny or semi-shade aspect, and may well be placed amidst bushes or trees. Its height is about 6 ft, and it flowers from June until the frosts. The bunches of berries make a fine decorative effect.

368 Polemonium coeruleum
(Jacob's Ladder)

This variety grows wild in European mountain districts. It prefers above all, cool and semi-sheltered places, and should be spaced 15 ins. apart. It will reach a height of 32 ins. It flowers from May to August, and suits beds of perennials. A white variety also exists.

369 Polemonium reptans

Originally from North America, it forms clumps or tufts. It reaches a foot in height. It blooms in June-July, and is grown like No. 368.

370 Polygonatum multiflorum
(Solomon's Seal)

The actual plant illustrated is probably a hybrid between P. multiflorum itself and P. officinale, and indeed is much greater in size than either of its parents. The height is from 32-36 ins., and it flowers from May to July. It prefers a rather cool and semi-sheltered spot, and also requires a place where it can increase freely. The flowers will last a long time in vases.

371   Polygonum bistorta *(Knotweed)*

This type comes from the Northern Hemisphere, and prefers damp situations. It serves as a ground cover, its foliage forming a carpet. It flowers from May to August, and grows 2 ft high. The flowers will last a long time. *P. bistorta superbum* is a very dazzling colour.

372   Potentilla *(Cinquefoil)* 'Gibson's Scarlet'

This comes originally from Nepal, and there are many varieties grown, of which 'Gibson's Scarlet' with its tall stems up to 2½ feet high, flowers from July to August. This plant prefers a good soil and a maximum of sun. It is easy to grow, and should be placed in the front row of beds of perennials or on rockeries.

373   Potentilla aurea

This often grows wild in the fields. It is free flowering, and goes excellently on rockeries. It grows 6 ins. high, and flowers from June to August. It is grown like the previous plant.

374   Potentilla 'Miss Willmott'

This variety, also from Nepal, is most free flowering. It is a perennial, suitable for rockeries, and flowers from June to September. It attains a height of 16 ins.

375-383   Primula

The primula family contains about 600 species, coming from cold or temperate regions of the Northern Hemisphere, and most of them are perennials. Many come from the mountains, and can grow under very severe conditions; though it is true that they only develop fully if certain conditions of growth and surrounding are satisfied. Generally speaking, primroses need aspects which are shaded for at least part of the day, and the majority of them like neutral or just slightly acid soil, which remains damp, but not soaked. Frosts without snow have disastrous effects upon some of them. It is therefore preferable to cover these plants during the winter. Primroses are best planted under deep-rooted trees, around bushes such as rhododendrons, or under pines, and in the shelter of hedgerows.

375   Primula beesiana

This comes originally from the Yunnan district of China. It is recommended as being especially suitable around ponds and ornamental water. It looks pretty grown among azaleas. It flowers from June-August, and attains a height of 2½ ft.

376   Primula denticulata

This plant comes originally from the Himalayas, and is often confused with *P. cashmeriana*. It is quite easy to grow, but is inclined to rot during too damp winters. It flowers in April and May, and it is especially suitable for rockeries and beds of perennial plants.

377   Primula florindae

Originally from Tibet, this flower reaches a height of 32 ins. It is recommended for growing around ponds and lakes, or among azaleas. It flowers from July to September.

378   Primula hortensis

Primula auricula, a type which grows wild in some parts, is surpassed in richness and quality of the flower by the hybrid, *Primula hortensis*. It is easy to grow all the same, and attains a height of from 6-8 ins. It flowers in April-May, and is agreeably perfumed. It is suitable for flower beds, rockeries and borders.

379   Primula japonica

This plant originates from Japan, and flowers in late August. The flowers appear from the bottom towards the top of the spikes. It grows from 12-15 ins.

380 Primula sieboldii

A native of Siberia, this plant forms quite thick clumps. From it has come a number of really good horticultural varieties. It is easy to grow, and attains a height of 10 ins., with flowers 2 ins. wide. Since it has a tendency of forming surface roots, it is wise to mulch the soil before the beginning of winter. The flowering period is May and June. This plant is suitable for rockeries.

381 Primula pulverulenta
'Helenae'

This is one of the most charming garden hybrids and one of the easiest to grow, being suitable for flower beds and for rockeries. Like No. 382 it is very precocious in flowering (March-May). It forms tufts, the flower stems being nearly 5 ins. high.

382 Primula
'Wanda'

This hybrid is not quite so sturdy as the previous one. It is of the same height.

383 Primula variabilis

There are, classed under the name of P. variabilis, a whole group of hybrid types, which are the result of work on their improvement over several centuries. These flowers open up from March to June, and attain a height of 4-6 ins. according to the variety. They are of bright and varied colours, and suitable for all uses.

384 Pulmonaria augustifolia
'Mrs. Moon' (Lungwort)

This plant is often to be found growing wild in woody districts. It is perennial, and one of the first plants to flower in spring. The flowers seem to turn colour from blue to red or vice versa. They prefer the shade and damp soil, and reach a height of 12 ins. They are suitable for flower beds, rockeries, and the banks of ponds.

385 Pulsatilla vulgaris

This plant grows wild throughout almost all Europe. It has the advantage of remaining decorative, after flowering, by the protraction of the feathery style which rises above the carpels. The foliage fades only when the seeds ripen. These flowers grow 6-8 ins. high, and they like the sun. Flowering is from April to June. They are suitable for rockeries, but old plants cannot be transplanted successfully.

386 Reseda odorata (Mignonette)

This plant comes originally from Egypt, and is an annual. The flowers are highly scented. Sow direct into flowering places. Flowers will appear from July-September, at a height of 12 ins.

387 Ranunculus asiaticus
(Turban Ranunculus)

There are various types of ranunculus both wild and cultured forms as seen in florists. shops. This one comes from Asia, and originally grew in China. It is a perennial having varied colours and preferring light soil which retains moisture, and a semi-sheltered position. They flower from May-June, and grow 10 ins. high; ideal for rockeries.

388 Ricinus communis
(Castor Oil Plant)

This plant comes originally from Africa in all probability, but it has long past been known in India, and is now cultivated in many countries. It is perennial when growing wild, but in our country it is grown as an annual. Very large in size, it reaches a height of 6-10 ft. in some places. A very well-known oil is extracted from its seeds. It is used to make up large groups with its leafy plants, and attracts attention by its unusual appearance in a garden. It should be sown in pots under glass. It needs good, rich soil, and a sunny, sheltered spot.

389 Rodgersia aesculifolia
(Bronze Leaf)

This plant comes from China. It needs growing in good soil, which retains moisture and is semi-shaded. It is perennial. The rich looking foliage is of a bronze colour. It flowers freely in July, attaining a height of 3 ft. The flowers are scented. This species should be placed in beds of perennials, or, better still, in big groups around ponds or lakes.

390 Rodgersia tabularis

If it is desired to give a really exotic looking touch to the make up of a garden, then this plant must not be missed. It is originally from China, and is perennial. It needs a deep, neutral soil, which retains moisture. It prefers above all a shaded spot, and may well be placed near houses with a northern aspect. The leaves attain a width of 3 ft, and it flowers in July.

391 Rudbeckia *(Coneflower)*
'*Herbstsonne*'

This variety is dedicated to the 17th century Swedish potanist, Claus Rudbeck. It needs a sheltered aspect. It reaches a height of 5-6 ft, and is suited to the back row of beds of perennials. Flowering in September and October, it is a good cutting flower.

392 Rudbeckia speciosa

Like the previous plant, this comes from North America, and it is easy to grow. It is most suitable for the front row of flower beds, where it establishes itself rapidly. It is extremely free flowering, but the blooms when cut do not last well. Flowering July-October.

393 Rudbeckia purpurea
'*The King*'

This plant requires a deep and well-manured ground, as well as a sheltered and sunny aspect. It flowers from August to October, the blooms being up to 5 ins. in diameter, produced on 5-6 ft stems. This variety should be placed at the back of flower beds or against walls.

394 Sagittaria sagittifolia
(Arrowhead)

This plant is frequently found in streams and similar places in Northern regions, and is a perennial, which grows well in Britain. It should be planted in ponds, pools or even in running water. It flowers from May to August, the height of the flowering stems being 3 ft.

395 Salpiglossis sinuata
(Scalloped Tube Tongue)

This variety comes originally from Chile, and is annual. It should be sown thinly and transplanted 8 ins. apart, but it does not attain its full development except in warm summers. It flowers from June to September. Suitable for beds and for cutting.

396 Salvia nemorosa

This sage with bluish-violet flowers blooms from June to August. The flowers are freely produced on long spikes. They are suitable for flower-beds, banks and semi-woodland places. There is also a white variety.

397 Salvia patens

This plant comes from Texas, and is

perennial but treated as annual in cold regions. The tuberous roots should be lifted and kept during the winter like dahlias. They should be planted under glass in February, then placed in pots and gradually hardened off and put in their beds in May. For preference, give them a warm and sunny aspect. They should be spaced 12 ins. apart, and will attain a height of 18-30 ins. They flower from August-October, and are most suitable for flower beds.

398 Salvia splendens

This variety comes originally from America, and our admirable garden sage plants are the result of improvements on the type. No flower is of such a brilliant red, and it is, moreover, a healthy plant, though it does require a warm and sheltered position. It should be spaced 12 ins. apart, and attains a height of 12 ins. It flowers all the summer, and is suitable for all uses.

399 Sanvitalia procumbens

This comes originally from Mexico, and is an annual. Seed should be sown in the flowering positions and the plants thinned to 4-6 ins. apart. Its spreading branches form a carpet, and the flowers appear from June to the end of summer. The height is 12 ins., and it is suitable for flower beds, borders and big rockeries.

400 Saponaria ocymoides
(Soapwort)

This plant grows wild in the mountains and on the limestone hills of Central and Southern Europe. It is perennial, and by its spreading stems forms low tufts of 4-8 ins. high. It requires a pebbly ground, and an aspect with the maximum of sun. It flowers abundantly from May to July. It is most suitable for rockeries.

401-405 Saxifraga *(Saxifrage)*

There are a considerable number of saxifrages in cultivation. Horticulturalists have adopted the division of them into five sections as proposed by botanists, so as to classify the varieties easily. However, nearly all saxifrages are mountain plants, though some like dry and pebbly soil, while others prefer light and shady spots.

401 Saxifraga lingulata superba

This variety is wild in some European countries and in France; it grows especially in the Provencal Alp districts. The form *superba* is more beautiful than the species as a whole. It prefers the sun or a half-shaded spot, and grows slowly. It grows to a height of 14 ins., and flowers appear from May-July.

402 Saxifraga apiculata

This charming spring flowering plant is extremely robust. It forms clumps, and grows fairly quickly, and is 4 ins. high. It flowers in March-April, and is especially suited for growing between stones or flagstones — especially red limestone — the dark green foliage making a beautiful, contrasting effect.

403 Saxifraga
'Beauty of Ronsdorf'

This forms rather loose tufts which have a mossy appearance. It grows rapidly and does not become pale in the sunlight like many varieties of the same group. It should be planted where it has plenty of room. Height 6 ins. *Saxifraga trifurcata* is a similar variety with white flowers, and also makes rapid growth.

404 Saxifraga cotyledon purpurata

This variety grows wild in the flinty mountains of Europe (the Alps and Pyrenees of France etc.). The variety *purpurata* is easier to grow than most of the group, which so often die after flowering. The flower stems will grow as much as 3 ft in height. It flowers from June to August, and lasts well when cut. The plants show to great effect on dry walls.

405 Saxifraga umbrosa
(London Pride)

This plant is robust and easy to grow, being as happy in the shade as right in the sun. It grows wild in the Western and Central Pyrenees. Numerous varieties exist, generally being shorter but with more vivid coloured flowers. The height is 12-20 ins. and the flowering period is from May to August. This flower is suitable for borders and for rockeries, as well as for walls and beds of perennials.

406 Scabiosa caucasica
(Caucasian Scabious)

This comes originally from the Caucasus, and is perennial. It has no special requirements and stands the drought well. It grows at its best in the full sunlight, and reaches 30-36 ins. in height. Flowering from June until the frosts, it looks well in mixed or in separate groups. It is also good for cutting and lasts well. Among the good varieties may be mentioned the following: 'Clive Greaves', blue; 'Miss Wilmott', white; and 'Moerheim Beauty', the darkest of the blue-violet types.

407 Scabiosa atropurpurea hybrida
(Sweet Scabious)

This dark purple garden flower comes originally from the Mediterranean countries, and is annual. It should be sown under glass at first, and planted out 8 ins. apart. It flowers from June until October, and attains a height of 32-36 ins. Well suited for cutting.

408 Schizanthus wisetonensis
(Butterfly Flower)

This plant comes originally from Chile, and is annual. It should be sown direct into flowering position, being thinned to 10 ins. apart. It prospers best in rich, well drained soil and a warm, sunny aspect, and reaches a height of 20 ins.; flowering in July-August. The flowers are curiously shaped and lightly perfumed with a strange scent. These plants are suitable for groups, and in mixed flower beds.

409 Scilla campanulata
(Spanish Bluebell)

Originally from Southern Europe, this plant is bulbous and free flowering. The bulbs should be planted 3-4 ins. deep, in September and October. Good sized groups are the most effective. They are quite happy in all soils, in sunny aspects or in the shade. They reach a height of 8-12 ins., and flower from April to June. They are useful in separate groups or flower beds.

410 Scilla siberica (Siberian Squill)

This flower comes originally from Southern Russia. It is one of the most delicate and finely coloured among spring flowers. The bulbs need planting in September or October at 1½-2 ins. deep, in grassy spots or on rockeries, for it prospers in all sorts of soil, in the sun or in semi-shady aspects. Flowering in March and April, they grow 4-9 ins. high. In suitable places the plants increase rapidly and in time cover large areas. It is one of the most lasting of our bulbous plants.

411-416 Sedum (Stonecrop)

This group of Sedums (or Orpins) contains about 500 species spread throughout the Northern Hemisphere particularly. All these plants have thick leaves with a smooth, waxy surface, and they can put up with strong sun and dry periods. Sedums are satisfied with shallow soil, and most of them like the sun. Some, however, prefer the shade. They are very useful for decorating rockeries.

411 Sedum acre

This plant grows wild in Europe, Western Asia, Siberia and North Africa, in rocky, pebbly and sandy places and on walls and roofs. It spreads easily, soon forming a carpet. It grows from 1½-2 ins. high, and flowers from May to August.

412 Sedum ewersii

This species comes from Mongolia, and is considered the finest of the Sedums. Though preferring the sun, it will grow almost anywhere. It attains a height of 2½ ins. and flowers from June to September. It is suitable for borders, rockeries and walls, and the first row of plants in mixed beds.

413 Sedum spectabile *'Brilliant'*

Originally from China, this plant requires good soil and a well drained and preferably sunny spot. It can be dug up and successfully transplanted when in full flower, and grows 12-16 ins. high. It flowers from August to October. It tolerates varying conditions, and can be used for planting on graves. The new hybrid of this species, named 'Carmen' is a little smaller but has flowers of a more sombre hue.

414 Sedum spathulifolium

This comes from North America and enjoys a soil both light and rich, in a sunny exposure. The whole plant has a kind of metallic brilliancy and is considered to be one of the finest of this group. The plant is low growing, reaching only 4-6 ins. in height, and it flowers in June.

415 Sedum spurium

This originates from the Caucasus and is a healthy growing plant, forming a floral carpet and easily becoming established in all districts. It can well replace grass in spots which are too dry, or so poor that graminaceous plants will not grow. It will put up with a slight trampling upon, and grows to a height of 5 ins., flowering from June to August. This is very suitable for rockeries, and the variety *splendens*, with its reddish-brown foliage and bright red flowers has all the good qualities of the group.

416 Sedum
'Munstead Dark Red'

Large flowered Stone-crop. The plant represented here is like the type *purpureum* of the *Sedum telephium*. It can grow in open or sheltered spots, woods and arbours, or even in dry and exposed positions.

417-420 Sempervivum *(Houseleek)*

As shown by its Latin name *Sempervivum* (Everlasting), this variety comprises types which are particularly healthy. A handful of earth on a little pebble is sufficient to enable them to live for years. In spite of this, if it is desired to produce strong plants, then it is necessary to provide them with a suitable surroundings. Houseleeks like sun, and are at home on rockeries. They will grow in the North of Europe, too, if they are covered in winter. The four kinds mentioned below flower during June and July.

417 Sempervivum arachnoideum

This grows wild particularly in the mountains of France, and the rosettes of small size (width of about ½ inch) are formed by the leaves being held together by small white strands, like a spider's web. This plant grows very slowly, and reaches 4-6 ins. in height. It is best to choose places where they can be admired close at hand.

418 Sempervivum heuffelii

This type is hybrid between *S. patens* and *S. reginae amaliae*. In dry spots and with rich soil, the rosettes assume a kind of metallic brilliancy, which makes them resemble echeverias, but they are not stoloniferous. They grow 6 ins. high.

419 Sempervivum funckii

The description of *Sempervivum funckii* used here is in reality much too abridged. This type belongs really to the whole group of *Sempervivum montanum*, which generally have pinkish flowers. The sempervivum, shown here, comes into the sub-species *Stiriacum Wettstein*, of which the variety *Brauni (Funck) Wettstein* has white or yellowish-white flowers.

420 Sempervivum tectorum alpinum

This grows wild in many places, and was once much used for growing on roofs. In France it is well-known as a popular remedy for burns and for corns. It is the most hardy type of all the Sempervivums. The flower stems reach 12 ins. in height. The example shown represents the sub-species *alpinum*.

421 Senecio przewalskii

This plant comes originally from Mongolia, and is a perennial. It likes a sunny exposure and fairly dry conditions. It increases by underground stolons, and it is for this reason that there are disadvantages in growing it in beds of perennials. Its leaves are very decorative. Growing 3 ft high, it flowers in July-August.

422 Sidalcea
' Elsie Hugh'

The varieties are much more abundant in flower than the species, and so are the favourites. In a well enriched site and sunny aspect, this plant reaches 3 ft in height. It flowers in July-August, and the florets are about an inch in diameter. Planted in small groups in beds of perennials, this plant is most effective. Other good varieties are 'Interlaken', a silvery-rose colour, and 'Crimson King', a crimson-red.

423-425 Solidago *(Golden Rod)*

Although it has not many requirements as to the nature of its soil, Golden Rod develops better in rich or semi-rich soil, just as it prefers full sunlight. It is better to divide and transplant it every two years, so as to obtain a really good flowering display. It is particularly decorative in flower beds, and an excellent cutting flower.

423 Solidago
'Golden Veil'

This grows 28 ins. high, and is very free flowering. The brilliant yellow flowers appear from August to October.

424 Solidago
'Golden Wings'

This variety has large panicles which are very elegant. It is late and flowers during September and October.

425 Solidago
'Perkeo'

This plant has both large and graceful flower-heads. It flowers in August-September, and is very much recommended. Height 2 ft.

426 Stachys macrantha

This plant comes from Western Asia, and is a perennial. It attains its full development in good soil which holds moisture. The height is 12-20 ins., and it flowers during June and July. Even after the flowering, the foliage remains decorative during the whole summer. It is suitable for mixed flower beds, and in separate clumps.

427 Stachys lanata *(Lamb's Ears)*

This plant comes from Eastern Europe and Western Asia, but has become fairly well naturalised in Britain. It attains a height of 12-20 ins., and flowers from June to September. It is suitable for the front row of beds and rockeries. It has silky, woolly leaves.

428 Stachys sinuata

This plant comes from the Mediterranean regions, and though perennial is usually grown as an annual. It is best sown under glass in March. It can then be transplanted later. Once hardened off it can be put into its place, at 10 ins. apart, in May. It is very decorative and long lasting, and is excellent for drying. These plants prefer a lightish, fairly rich soil, and a sunny aspect. It grows from 16-24 ins. high, and is especially recommended for cutting.

429 Statice latifolia (Limonium)
(Sea Lavender)

This type comes from Eastern Europe and is a perennial. It grows in all soils even the most rough and stony, though it prefers a sunny position. Growing 24-32 ins. high it flowers from July to September. It is suitable for flower beds, rockeries and also for cutting, and is one of the best flowers for drying.

430-437 Tagetes *(Marigold)*

This plant comes from Mexico, and is annual. African marigolds, as they are known, can be sown where they are to flower, but those plants which have been sown under glass develop better

and flower earlier. The larger varieties should be spaced 12-16 ins. apart, whereas the dwarf varieties need a spacing of only 6-10 ins. All need a rich soil, and a warm and sunny aspect. *Tagetes patula*, the double flowered dwarf marigold, can be moved even when in full flower, and will serve for filling up spaces in flower beds or on rockeries. The tall types should be placed in clumps in flower beds, leaving the smaller types for the borders. They last when cut, but their perfume is unpleasant to some people, and so those types with but little scent or even none at all are the most in demand.

All the tagetes or marigolds are free flowering, and their exact colour depends to a great extent on both the weather and the temperature. For instance, during wet and cold summers, their flowers are lighter in hue. The flowering of the small sized varieties begins at the opening of June, whereas that of the larger sizes will begin July. They last until well into September, often until October.

430 Tagetes patula nana
'Robert Beist'

This dwarf marigold is 14 ins. high, and suitable for clumps.

431 Tagetes patula nana
lemon-yellow

This is particularly free flowering. Its height is 14 ins. It is indispensable for flower beds and borders.

432 Tagetes erecta
'Yellow Supreme'

This is another double marigold, and suitable for garden decoration and for cutting. Its height reaches 24 ins.

433 Tagetes erecta
'Guinea Gold'

The height of this African marigold is

28 ins., and it is suitable for beds of flowers and for cutting.

434 Tagetes patula
'Naughty Marietta'

This plant has a height of 16 ins., with petals distinctly larger than many of the older varieties, on which it is an improvement.

435 Tagetes patula
'Harmony' (French Marigold)

This is a beautiful flower and very free growing; it reaches 18 ins. in height, and it is well suited for clumps.

436 Tagetes *'Flash'*

This plant has a height of 16 ins. The flowers are regular in size. It is one of the best for beds and borders.

437 Tagetes signata pumila

The height of this plant is only 10 ins., It is very free flowering, and suitable for borders and rockeries. It is sometimes known as *T. tenuifolia pumila.*

438 Thalictrum aquilegifolium

This plant grows wild in the mountains of Europe. It thrives in shady or semi-shaded spots, in soil which retains moisture and which is neutral or slightly sour. The petalloid sepals fall early, but the stamens, which are very decorative, last a long time. The height is about 3 ft, and the flowering period is May to July. It does well growing near water and among rhododendrons, and other shrubs, and is an excellent plant for beds of perennials.

439 Thalictrum dipterocarpum
(Meadow Rue)

This variety comes from East Asia, and is 5 ft high. It is light and graceful looking, and is grown as the previous variety. The flowering period is June to August.

440 Thymus serphyllum splendens
(Thyme)

The type grows wild in Europe, North Africa, and throughout a great part of Asia, and is most abundant in flower. The perfume is very pleasant, and the flowers appear from June to September. Its height is 1¼ ins., and its growth and use are the same as No. 441.

441 Thymus lanuginosus

This kind of thyme grows wild in the mountains of Central Europe, in the Alps, and French Pyrenees. The horticultural forms are particularly decorative if they are allowed to spread. They are generally grown, however, for their foliage, which is covered with greyish down. The flowers come only to full exposure in meagre soil and in full sunlight. Its height reaches only ¾ in., and the flowering is in July and August. It is showy when grown over wide areas, and on rockeries.

442 Tradescantia virginiana
(Spiderwort)

This plant comes originally from North America. It thrives in soil which retains moisture and also a sunny exposure. It grows 2 ft high, and the flowering, which begins in May, goes on throughout the whole summer. It is bestused in or near the front row of perennial flower beds.

443 Trollius europaeus superbus
(Globe Flower)

Will grow freely in moist soil. The varieties now available are the result of the crossing of several species. They should be placed preferably near bushy or leafy plants which flower at the end of summer, and which will cover the spaces left by the Globe Flowers when the blooms are over. They like the sun or semi-shade, and a rich, moisture-retaining soil. They look lovely in beds of perennials, near shrubs, and on the banks of water where their yellow or orange-yellow flowers show up well. The variety 'Earliest of All' flowers in May. The width of its flowers is 1¾ ins., and their height 24 ins. It is much appreciated for cutting, although the flowers do not last well.

444 Trollius
'Orange Globe'

This hybrid Orange Globe-Flower grows 28 ins. high. It blooms freely during May and June. The diameter of the flowers is 2 ins.

445 Trollius
'Prichards Giant'

This plant reaches a height of 32-36 ins., and has giant flowers up to 2½ ins. in width. It is the best of the group for cutting.

446-449 Tropaeolum
(Nasturtium)

The garden kinds come originally from Central and Southern America. They should not have too rich a soil, nor too great a quantity of nitrogenous manure, which causes the increase of the foliage to the detriment of the flowers. They prefer a sunny aspect, though they will grow in semi-shaded conditions. They are annual, and the seed should be sown an inch deep. It is necessary for a good variety to have flowers with fairly long stalks, well above the foliage, and those that are mentioned here satisfy this requirement. They flower from May and continue blooming all the summer. They can be used for borders, balcony boxes, walls and fences, as well as for banks and around gateways, and also as cut flowers.

446 Tropaeolum majus

Semi-high, this type has flowers which are plainly visible above the foliage.

447 Tropaeolum, double

This is a quite recent introduction, and semi-trailing. It has indeed all the qualities which can be required of a nasturtium.

448 Tropaeolum
'King of Tom Thumb'

This is a dwarf and bushy variety. The foliage is less tall and darker than that of the other varieties. It is particularly well suited for vases and window-boxes.

449 Tropaeolum peregrinum

This variety climbs, and is annual. It grows very rapidly too, and reaches a height of 12 ft during the summer. It flowers from July till November, and grows similarly to the other nasturtiums.

450-484 Tulipa (Tulip)

Tulips grow in Europe, North Africa, Western and Central Asia as far as Japan. Many garden tulips come originally from Turkey and from Asia Minor. Two meanings are suggested for the word Tulipa: (1) It is suggested that the word derives from the Persian word for these plants, 'Thoulyban'; (2) The idea has often been put forward that it is a derivation of 'Tulbend', or 'Dulbend', a Turkish word, meaning 'turban', which it is said these flowers resemble. It was an Austrian diplomat, Augier Ghislain de Busbecq, who first brought them into Europe, and to whom we owe their first botanical description (1554). They were classified by Linnaeus in 1752. Right from the beginning of their cultivation, tulips were highly appreciated. There were in Holland, for instance, huge speculations on these plants and substantial sums were paid for the purchase of a bulb of a new variety. People went as far as to buy bulbs which did not yet exist. This kind of speculation was ended by the financial slump of 1652 with its world wide repercussions.

Tulips can be classified in the following manner:

Single Dwarf Tulips: These are the earliest and their colours are bright and definite, but the flowers are, relatively, short living. Their normal time of flowering is in April-May, but among them are some which can be forced to flower in December.

Double Early Tulips: These are a little later than the previous type, but last much longer in flower. In this group are some of the best bedding varieties.

Peony (or Bull-finch) Tulips: Late flowering, but giant double flowers and lasting. Excellent both for flower beds and for cutting.

Darwin Tulips: Flower in April and May, growing 24-36 ins. high. They are grand flowers of noble appearance, and excellent for cutting. They are perhaps the very best for banks or groups.

Cottage Tulips: These have single flowers, and they bloom after the ordinary single early tulips. The Cottage type are excellent for lawns.

Mendel Tulips: A recently introduced group, they have large single flowers, perfectly formed. They are a little earlier, and shorter than the Darwins.

Breeder Tulips: This is an old Dutch group which has again come back into favour. They are single, of medium height, and stiff growing.

Triumph Tulips: This group is most attractive. It flowers just one week earlier than the Darwins, and are rather shorter than the latter. The large, single flowers last well.

Parrot Tulips: These are the latest of the hybrid varieties. They have long slender stalks, and their flower heads are fringed and laciniated, while their colours are both br ght and var ed.

They are the best for planting among shrubs.

Lily-Flowered Tulips: These have graceful stalks, and the flowers are of elegant form. They flower rather late.

Tulip Species: This group comprises a large number of botanical types and their hybrids, of various form, size and colour. Some are early, others mid-season or late flowering, and some are among the earliest known tulips. These plants prefer a more or less alkaline soil, rich, but not too freshly manured. The make up of the soil is of little importance; sand, loam or clay suits tulips, though a lightish ground is easier to work. Plant the bulbs in September or October, about 4-6 ins. deep, and the biggest bulbs available should be chosen. As the rooting of tulips is rather weak, it is better not to plant them near shrubs or trees.

After flowering is finished, the bulbs should not be lifted until the leaves have died down, and the bulbils which develop round the main bulbs should be lifted first. They should be kept in the dry during the summer, until ready for planting again in the autumn; or they may be left in the ground.

450 Tulipa fosteriana
'Red Emperor'

This has a height of 18 ins., and is early. It has very large flowers, and it prefers a sheltered aspect and well drained soil.

451 Tulipa Kaumfanniana

This tulip is no doubt one of the earliest. It grows 8 ins. high and is often called the water lily tulip. It is particularly well suited for rockeries, and the bulbs can be left in the soil for several years.

452 Tulipa praestans
'Fusilier'

This is early, and reaches a height of

14 ins. Its stem carries 3 or 4 flowers. It looks well growing among perennial plants.

453 Tulip
single, 'Ibis'

The height of this variety is 14 ins. It is very showy and easily grown.

454 Tulip
single, 'Keiserskroon'

This also grows about 14 ins. high, and is of a very beautiful appearance both in beds and when growing in lawns.

455 Tulip
single, 'Couleur Cardinal'

This single flowering variety grows 14-15 ins. high, and shows up particularly well against light backgrounds.

456 Tulip
single, 'Yellow Prince'

This grows 12 ins. high, and is the earliest among the yellows. It fades easily in the sunlight.

457 Tulip
single, 'Brilliant Star'

This variety is 10 ins. high. It is the best variety for forcing.

458 Tulip
double, 'Peach Blossom'

This double variety attains a height of 12 ins. It is quite a dazzling variety placed when against a sombre background. It is suitable for forcing.

459 Tulip
double, 'Therose'

This double yellow Tulip is similar to the previous one, differing only in colour. It is sometimes known as 'Tea Rose'.

460 Tulip
double, 'Orange Nassau'

A double early, growing 12 ins. high It is suitable for forcing, and should be placed in groups.

461 Tulip
Darwin, 'Clara Butt'

This variety grows 20 ins. high, and is relatively early. It is well suited for banks of flowers, and also for cutting.

462 Tulip
Darwin, 'Demeter'

This flower has a height of 2 ft; it is very suitable for flower beds and borders.

463 Tulip
Darwin, 'Golden Age'

This also reaches 2 ft. It should be noted that it is the only really good yellow variety among the Darwins.

464 Tulip
Cottage, 'Aristocrat'

This grows 28 ins. high. It flowers for a long time, and is suitable for growing in groups, and for cutting.

465 Tulip
Darwin, 'William Pitt'

This also grows 28 ins. high, and is rather late; it has giant-sized flowers of elegant form, with a strong stem.

466 Tulip
Darwin, 'City of Haarlem'

Growing 28 ins. high, this is a robust plant. It is splendid in every way; suitable for groups.

467 Tulip
Darwin, 'Scarlet Leader'

This has a height of 2 ft. It is fairly early, and suitable both for flower beds and for groups.

468 Tulip

Darwin, 'The Bishop'

This variety grows 28 ins. high. Its colouring is extremely unusual and not suitable for all purposes. It makes a fine effect seen against a good lawn.

469 Tulip

Darwin, 'Pride of Zwanenburg'

This grows 2½ ft high. It flowers late, and is much valued for planting in groups.

470 Tulip

Darwin, 'Zwanenburg'

This flower reaches 28 ins., and is also late. It is one of the best among the white varieties.

471 Tulip

Darwin, 'Afterglow'

Growing 22 ins. high, it is early, and suitable for groups. The colouring is rather unusual in Darwins.

472 Tulip

Darwin, 'La Tulipe Noire'

This tulips reaches 2 ft. It is one of the most remarkable of all varieties, if only for the simple fact that it was long judged impossible to produce a black flower. It is more curious than beautiful.

473 Tulip

Cottage, 'Golden Harvest'

The height of this variety is 2 ft. It is very reliable in flowering, and an excellent variety for flower beds.

474 Tulip

Cottage, 'Louis XIV'

This grows 2 ft high. On strong stems, it produces large, well formed flowers.

475 Tulip

Cottage, 'Princess Margaret Rose'

This tulip grows 20 ins. high. It has pretty flowers. It is suitable for grouping in beds, and lasts well when cut.

476 Tulip

Cottage, 'Telescopium'

Another variety which grows 20 ins. high. It is fairly early and a good garden variety.

477 Tulip

Cottage, 'Orange Wonder'

This flower grows 2 ft high. It looks well placed among shrubs.

478 Tulip

Cottage, 'Dillenburg'

This also grows 2 ft high. It is rather stiff and should be grown with low growing plants at the base of the stems.

479 Tulip

Cottage, 'Mona Lucia'

Growing 2 ft high, this is a Swedish creation. The flower is very large and well formed and can be thoroughly recommended. It is most suitable for flower beds.

480 Tulip

Lily flowered, 'Captain Fryatt'

This is a late flowering tulip which grows 2 ft high. It has large flowers of unusual form. Excellent for the garden.

481 Tulip

Lily flowered, 'Mrs. Moon'

Another late tulip growing 2 ft high. Its bright flowers are very long lasting.

482 Tulip

Parrot, 'Violet Queen'

This is also late. Its height is 22 ins. It is undoubtedly the most beautiful of the group.

483 Tulip

Parrot, 'Sunshine'

This plant grows 20 ins. high. Its flowers are large, and it is excellent for the garden.

484 Tulip   *Parrot, 'Red Champion'*

This also grows 20 ins. high. It is a beautiful flower, and the best of the reds in this group.

485 Verbascum phoeniceum *'Pink Domino' (Mullein or Aaron's Rod)*

This grows wild in Central and Southern Europe, as well as in Southern and Western Asia. It is biennial or perennial, although often grown as annual. It likes an open and sunny aspect, and prefers dry and rather stony soil. Its position moreover should not be damp in winter. It grows 3-4 ft high, and flowers in July and August. It is recommended for flower beds and for gardens of the wild type, and looks well in cottage gardens. As these plants often die after flowering, it should be noted that they are easily resown, and young plants are the strongest growing. If they are to be grown as perennials, these must be covered in winter.

486 Verbascum olympicum
     (Olympian Mullein)

This type is wild in almost all Europe. It is treated either as a biennial or perennial. The leaves are covered with a whitish down. The growth and use are the same as for the former variety.

487-491 Verbena *(Vervain)*

Garden verbenas are ancient plants of obscure origin. It is certain however, that their parents came from South America. They should be sown under glass in February and later placed in a garden frame. This will ensure that they are hardened off for planting out in May. They should be spaced 10-12 ins. apart. They flower from July and last until October or until the frosts come. They grow in any good soil but prefer a sunny exposure. Always distinct and tidy looking, verbena plants have many uses and grow well in flower beds, in

separate groups, balconies, and in window-boxes. They are also attractive as cut flowers.

487 Verbena
     'Defiance'

This variety is 16 ins. high, and is of bushy habit. It flowers early in July.

488 Verbena
     'Royal Blue'

This is 18 ins. high, and is really a greyish-mauve colour.

489 Verbena candidissima

This plant grows only 10 ins. high, and is one of a group of dwarf hybrids. It gives an excellent effect, placed in front of brightly coloured flowers.

490 Verbena venosa
     hybrids

Grows 16-20 ins. high and flowers from July to October.

491 Verbena
     'Dannebrog'

This garden variety grows from 10-16 ins. high. It is a good type for the flower bed, and blooms early.

492 Veronica incana

The Veronica family comprises about 250 species, coming principally from cold countries. A certain number have been grown in gardens however, for centuries past. *Veronica incana*, which comes originally from the Ukraine, can stand drought and has no special requirements as to soil. It prefers a sunny situation. Its height attains 18 ins., and it flowers in June-July. It is especially suitable for flower beds of perennials.

493 Veronica spicata
     'Erika'

This type thrives in all types of soil and

likes full sunlight. The spikes are a foot high, the actual flower-head being 5 or 6 ins. It flowers from June to August, and is best placed in the front row of beds of perennials.

494 Veronica longifolia

This plant comes from Northern and Central Europe, as well as from Greece and the Caucasus, and is also well-known in Japan, France and Britain. It is perennial, easy to grow, and likes either the sun or the semi-shade, and attains a height of 32 ins. It flowers from June to August, and is suitable for flower beds and for cutting.

495 Veronica teucrium
'Royal Blue'

This is a beautiful flower and easily grown. Height 16 ins. It is suitable for flower beds and for cutting.

496 Viola cornuta 'Hansa'

This variety grows wild in the pasture-lands of the Alps and has long been known in this country. This variety represents an improvement on the old type of 'Gustaf Wermig' and like the latter, it has the advantage of flowering the whole summer. It should be planted in the spring and needs a spacing of 12 ins. It grows 6-8 ins. high. It is one of the best perennial plants suitable for border edgings and rockeries, as well as for covering ground in flower beds of perennials.

497 Viola gracilis 'Lord Nelson'
(Olympian Violet)

This species comes from the Balkans. It requires rich, porous land and a maximum of sunlight. It grows 6 ins. high, begins to flower at the end of the winter, and goes on until the beginning of August. It has similar uses to No. 496, but is less sturdy.

498 Viola hybrida
'Aurora'

People often, quite wrongly, include the hybrid violas with the 'Cornuta' Group. They are in fact more difficult to grow, and require a light, well drained soil, and a sunny aspect. They are suitable for edging borders, and flower from May to August.

499 Viola hybrida
'Jackanapes'

This is a rather capricious variety, but once established it proves very satisfactory. It is of the same habit, and has the same uses as the previous mentioned violas. It grows 6 ins. high, and flowers over a long period.

500 Viola odorata (Violet)

This is an indigenous plant which does well in ordinary garden soil. It likes the shade, and grows 4 ins. high. It flowers in March and April, or even earlier if the situation is sheltered.

501-507 Viola tricolor
(Heart's Ease)

Garden pansies are the result of the crossing between two species of violas, or of the crossing of one of the hybrids thus obtained with another species. Pansies are classified in several groups. The Hiemalis or winter-flowering sorts are very early. Those in the Trimardeau Section are next to flower. These, however, have been largely ousted from the market by the 'Roggli' pansies, with their huge flowers and intense clear colours, which were previously unknown.

The pansy is generally grown as biennial: seed should be sown in June and July. They are also treated as annual plants when they should be sown in the spring. Flowering begins in June and goes on throughout the whole summer. Pansies can grow in all soils with a sunny exposure, and may also be transplanted without harm. They are suitable for grouping in beds or for border edgings, and may be used for window-boxes. They are relatively long lasting in vases when cut. Nearly all have a sweet and agreeable perfume.

501 Viola tricolor
'Jupiter' Large flowered Pansy

The height of this pansy is 6 ins., and it is early flowering belonging to the Hiemalis group. It looks well mixed with other varieties.

502 Viola tricolor
'Iskungen' Large flowered Pansy

This large flowered pansy also grows 6 ins. high, and is another variety in the hiemalis group.

503 Viola tricolor
Large flowered Pansy

Another example of a large flowered winter pansy. It should be grown with the yellow variety.

504 Viola tricolor
'Mars' Large flowered Pansy

This is yet a further variety in the hiemalis group.

505 Viola tricolor
Large flowered Pansy

A reliable variety. A favourite colour in the hiemalis group.

506 Viola tricolor
Large flowered Pansy

This is also a large flowered, early pansy and undoubtedly one of the best of the hiemalis group in the dark blue tones.

507 Viola tricolor 'Roggli'
Large flowered Pansy.

This large flowered pansy has the advantage that it flowers over a very long season, and has a wide colour range. The flowers are over 3 ins. in diameter. It is excellent either for grouping or for flower borders. There are various named varieties with flowers of yellow, brown, claret or deep blue.

508 Viscaria splendens, flore pleno

This is the double variety of the lychnis or viscaria which grows wild. It is a perennial, and needs ordinary good soil and a sunny aspect. It grows 12-16 ins. high, and flowers during June and July. It should be placed in small groups in the front row of the herbaceous border.

509 Yucca filamentosa
(Adam's Needle)

This plant comes from the United States. It requires a warm and sunny exposure, and prefers light soil which is well drained and rich. The flowering period begins in June or July and lasts right into October. The flower stems sometimes reach a height of 8 ft or more. It may be planted near groups of trees, on the south side of large rockeries, or on its own, on, or near a lawn, or on the edge of a paved walk.

510-511 Zinnia *(Youth-and-Age)*

Originally from Mexico, zinnias are, in spite of their stiff habit of growth, one of our most popular plants. Seed should be sown under frames in April, hardened off and put into their places in May or June in a warm and sunny situation. They need rich soil and a spacing of 10-12 ins. The flowering period begins in June and will continue right throughout the summer. The colours are both vivid and varied. They are suitable for flower beds and borders, and are splendid for cutting

510 Zinnia elegans *mixed*

These attain a height of 20-36 ins., the diameter of the flowers being 3 ins. or more. They should be placed in groups, either alone or among other subjects. The variety 'California Giant' has flowers 4-6 ins. wide.

511 Zinnia
'*Lilliput*' *mixed*

The height of these is only 10-16 ins., but they are very bushy. The flowers, though smaller, are more numerous. It is a suitable type for flower beds, and for rockeries.

INDEX OF LATIN NAMES

The numbers given refer to pages. From 5 to 132: pictures.
From 134 to 193: textpages.

INDEX OF ENGLISH NAMES

In the Same Series: